Beyond Piety

Beyond Piety

The Christian Spiritual Life, Justice, and Liberation

GILBERTO CAVAZOS-GONZÁLEZ, OFM

WIPF & STOCK · Eugene, Oregon

BEYOND PIETY
The Christian Spiritual Life, Justice, and Liberation

Wipf & Stock
An Imprint of Wipf and Stock Publishers
199 W. 8th Ave., Suite 3
Eugene, OR 97401
www.wipfandstock.com

ISBN 13: 978-1-60899-509-7

Manufactured in the U.S.A.

Dedicated to
the members of
La Tropa de Cristo
(Our Lady of Angels Catholic Church, San Antonio, TX)
(1987–1993),
especially
Brenda Martínez-Beltran, Hijinio Cortez,
Enrique González, Timothy Rodríguez
and Frank Anthony Gonzales.

Dedicación:
En recuerdo cariñoso de mi sobrina
Larissa Irazemma Cavazos
(1982–2005)

Heart of a Poet

One needs the heart of a poet;
a heart that welcomes,
a heart that receives,
a heart that assimilates.

One needs the heart of a poet;
a heart that paints
the most intense of emotions.
A heart that gathers humanity
and engraves it with pen and paper.
A heart that cannot fake anything;
but sings and relates it all.

One needs the heart of a poet;
a heart as big as a seed,
a heart as small as a torrent,
a heart, that is natural and alive.

One needs the heart of a poet;
a heart that knows how to enjoy life
and cry over pain.
A heart that stimulates hearts
and gives them words.
A heart that loves and desires
with gratitude.
A heart like yours. . . . Like mine.

Gilberto Cavazos-González, OFM
English translation of my poem "Cuore di Poeta"
written in Rome, April 1997

Contents

Sidebars

Tables

Preface

CHRISTIAN SPIRITUALITY IS NOT simply about devotional practices or religiosity. Moving beyond piety we find that Christian spirituality is primarily and most emphatically about life in the Holy Spirit. More than piety, Christian life is a vocation, a calling in the world, a life project or share in God's mission. Hopefully most Christians know this, even though we are not always attentive to it. All too often we relegate Christian spirituality to pious practice, prayerful devotion, evangelization, religious buildings, and "spiritual" leaders as if the Gospel message of Jesus had nothing to do with our home life, our work, our recreation, and our role in society. This is a common mistake and one we need to outgrow.

At the age of twelve, Jesus thought that to do his Father's will he had to be in the temple discussing God's Word with the teachers of the Law. Like the young Jesus, many Christians seem to believe that sharing in God's mission means prayer, Bible study, and going to church. Luckily for Jesus, Mary and Joseph took him home, where thanks to their efforts and instruction he grew in wisdom and grace (Luke 2:49). Some eighteen years later, besides in synagogues and the temple, Jesus did his Father's mission and will in the fields, on fishermen's boats, at dinner parties, and in the market place with ordinary people and even public sinners.

My hope in writing this book is to help my brothers and sisters in Christ grow in wisdom and grace by coming to a better understanding of the Christian spiritual life and how it relates to justice and liberation. Like the young Jesus, you and I need to mature in our view of how to best serve God and share in his mission of creating, saving, and sanctifying the world. God calls us to be Christian where we are every day of the week—in our homes, at work, at school, at play—and not just at church on Sunday.

This book grows out of my course on Christian Spiritual Formation for seminarians and lay ministers at Catholic Theological Union and my course on *La vida espiritual Cristiana* for the deacon candidates and their wives in the *Instituto de Liderazgo Pastoral* of the Archdiocese of Chicago. As a result I owe a debt of gratitude to the students who for the last ten years have participated in those two courses. As a professor, I find that I learn a lot from my students when I am teaching a course, because while they have one professor, I have a room full of teachers. Every time I have taught both these classes, I have been edified and educated by the lived examples my students share in class. So my first thank you and *muchas gracias* goes to them.

More recently my work on the Christian spiritual life has been enhanced by my participation in a group of Catholic and Protestant theology professors and formation directors who gathered in the summer of 2009 to reflect on "The Christians' Callings in the World." I would like to thank these professors and formators from Fuller Theological Seminary, Princeton Theological Seminary, Yale Divinity School, Luther Theological Seminary, and Catholic Theological Union, for their work and insights.

Over the years I have learned a lot about being Christian from my brothers and sisters in the Lord. I thank God for all of them, especially the members of La Tropa de Cristo, a youth evangelization team I founded at Our Lady of Angels Church in San Antonio Texas in the 1980s. Their stories, their faith, and their preaching taught me a lot about moving beyond piety and into concrete action on behalf of the Gospel. I am also particularly grateful to Alexander Gaitan, Carmen Nanko-Fernández, Jaime Bascuñan, Gary Riebe-Estrella, Luigi Miranda, Fernando Harris, Dennis Joseph, JoKay Joseph, Arturo Ocampo, OFM, and David Rodríguez, OFM, for their love and encouragement especially while writing this book. *Diosito les conceda paz y todo bien* or, as I like to say, *pax et bonum amplexumque.*

My debt of gratitude would not be complete without giving *mil gracias y muchisimo cariño* to the people who taught me to live and love in the Lord, la familia Cavazos-González. *Deseo agradecer en especial a mis padres Gilberto y Emma y con mis hermanos Sergio, José Luis, Gustavo y sus esposas Norma, Herminia e Yvonne.* I also want to thank my sobrinas y sobrinos Larissa, Sergio, Eliana, José Luis, Gilberto, and Emma. *Los quiero mucho. Que Diosito me los bendiga.*

Fray Gilberto, OFM

Introduction

Describing Christian Spirituality

I LOVE THE SOUND of the wind. It seems to sing amid the rustling leaves as it blows between the branches of a tree. It whooshes between buildings with a sometimes-gentle, sometimes-piercing whistle. It whispers over tranquil meadows and majestic hills. I especially love to hear it moan as it crashes waves of the sea into the sand of the seashore. Jesus claims that as the wind blows, so it is with those born of the Spirit (John 3:8). The Spirit or wind blows where it wills, with no one knowing where it comes from or where it is going; yet you can hear its voice. Those people born of the Spirit become the rustling leaves, strong buildings, crashing waters, tranquil meadows, and majestic hills where the wind of the Spirit becomes a song, a whistle, a whisper, or a moan; where the human spirit proclaims its spirituality.

Spirituality is a fascinating and often misunderstood subject. Thousands upon thousands of books and magazine articles treat the topic of spirituality. Doing a word search on the Internet leads you to 29,000,000 results for the word *spirituality* (32,800,000 for "Christian Spirituality" and 60,600,000 for "spiritual").[1] A cursory look at these references reveals that people understand spirituality as either something "religious" or something just the opposite of religious. "I'm spiritual, not religious" has become an all too common catch phrase. Unfortunately for many people, spirituality deals exclusively with the inner world or interiority as opposed to the real or outer world. For many, it has to do with esoteric or new age cults. And for many Christians, it is nothing more than traditional piety and devotional practices.

---

1. These results are from bing.com (http://www.bing.com) on April 23, 2010.

Spirituality in general is often thought of as contrary to matters of the body and the world. To be spiritual is considered an escape from the secular or secularized world we live in, especially from all its socio-political and economic woes. Often it is seen as a way of turning to a higher power (God, if you will) in order to leave behind the iron grip of religion to move into a "new age" of private enlightenment or *gnosis*. Spirituality as a Christian experience is often seen as ineffective in dealing with the "real" events of *lo cotidiano*[2] (see sidebar).

> **LO COTIDIANO**
>
> *Lo cotidiano* and *cotidianidad* are the daily; the quotidian; the commonplace and routine nature of day to day living as well the occasional highlight of something wonderful and the unwelcome reality of sorrow and difficulties that sometimes occur in daily living. These two terms are used by many Latino/a (Latino and Latina) theologians in the United States in reference to where theological reflection and discussion need to take place. Christian spirituality and God-talk take into serious consideration our *cotidianidad*.

Christian spirituality needs to be liberated from false or limited understandings that seek to place it dualistically in contrast with material reality. It needs to be liberated from those who would keep the Spirit of Jesus in a Bible, a tabernacle, a rosary, or a retreat center. If the Spirit of Christ that dwells in each Christian is to sing, whistle, whisper, or moan effectively in the Church and in the world, it must be allowed to blow away the chains that keep people poor, bound, blind, and imprisoned. Christian spirituality is about traditional piety and devotional practices, but these are worthless if it is not also about justice, peace, and liberation. To live our Gospel calling as disciples of Jesus in the world we need a clearer understanding of Christian spirituality as a liberating spirituality.

In this book, I would like to clarify the Christian concept of spirituality, not by offering yet another definition of the term, but rather by looking at what spirituality is and how it is put into practice in our *cotidiano*. This is a book about growing in our faith as Christians so that we can truly live our spirituality as a life guided by the Spirit of Jesus. But first I would like to give you a very short history and a description of the term.

2. Cf. Nanko-Fernández, "Lo Cotidiano," 158–60.

SHORT HISTORY OF THE TERM

"Spirituality," it has been said, is an ancient yet novel discipline. And even though the term was coined within Christianity, it is a much older and wider phenomenon or human experience than just Christian spirituality. In one way or another, humanity has always sought the vitality and inspiration of spirituality.

St. Paul encourages the faithful to be "spiritual," but you will not find the word *spirituality* in the Sacred Scriptures. The English word *spirituality* has only been around since the first half of the twentieth century. No one knows for sure who coined the original Latin word *spiritualitas*. Scholars of spirituality or spiritualogians[3] (see sidebar) believe that the term most likely came from the fifth-century French bishop Faustus who coined it in a letter urging a newly baptized reader to *age ut in spiritualitatis* or rather to "act . . . in spirituality" (in a spiritual manner).[4] From that time on, Christians spoke of acting out or living one's Holy Spirit-filled life with the Latin word *spiritualitas*. Originally, *spiritualitas* was something that all baptized Christians had and were expected to grow in. Eventually, spirituality became the domain of special Christians far removed from ordinary Christian life. In the Late Middle Ages, Scholastic theology came to see *spiritualitas* as relegated to emotional interiority and "special experiences," separated from *lo cotidiano*, public life, and social praxis.[5]

> ### SPIRITUALOGIANS
>
> I coined this word a few years ago to distinguish theologians who specialize in the field of spirituality from "theologians of spirituality," who work in the field of spiritual theology.
>
> Spiritualogians are scholars dedicated to the advancement of the academic discipline known as spirituality.

---

3. Cf. Cavazos-González, "Cotidianidad Divina," para. 8.

4. The letter was written to a certain Tesifonte. The setting for the phrase is this: "Thanks to grace, O worthy and beloved brother, any reason for tears has been taken from you, therefore act, guard yourself, run, hurry. *Act in such a way as to grow in spirituality.* Take care not to lose through imprudence and negligence the good you have received. Run so as not to forget, Hurry so as to better understand. . . . While we still have time, we sow in the Spirit so as to gather a harvest of spiritual things." Cf. Secondin, *Spiritualitá in dialogo*, 31. Translation of the Italian text is mine.

5. I would be remiss if I did not mention that at the same time *spiritual* in the juridical sense of the term came to be used to refer to those things or people belonging to the Church or consecrated for the service of God.

Although a French author in the thirteenth century translated the word *spiritualituas* into French, it was not until the 1500s that *spiritualitas* was considered something that the laity could understand, when Franciscan Friar Mariano da Firenze translated it into Italian for his work *The Spiritual Life*. This was soon followed by the Spanish translation into *espiritualidad*. With these translations *spiritualitas* began to undergo a slow and gradual democratization process by which spirituality eventually came to be understood as something that is part and parcel of all human beings not just a Christian elite.

DESCRIPTION OF SPIRITUALITY

In the 1920s *spiritualitas* was finally translated into the English "spirituality" and used in a four-volume translation of a work by the French theologian Pierre Pourrat on Christian Spirituality. As more and more books and conferences began to use the word *spirituality* in their titles, it slowly entered popular language in the latter half of the twentieth century. The widespread use of the word *spirituality* in a variety of contemporary languages has led many non-Christians to use the word as well. What began as a Christian word has become a word used by many of the world's religions and "religious" movements to mean a variety of things depending on their relationship to the material world. Many contemporary spiritualogians are trying to help us understand what spirituality is in Christian terms. Their study has led to the division of talk about spirituality into four categories of understanding: human reality, personal experience, communal traditions, and academic discipline.

Human Reality

"We do not become spiritual! We are spiritual."[6] God breathed *ruah* (spirit/life/breath) into all of us (Gen 2:7) therefore all humans are spiritual beings (*Homo spiritualis*). In other words, spirit is very much a part of who we are as humans. This ontological reality is part and parcel of Christian anthropology, because, as image of God (*imago Dei*), the human being is "at once corporeal and spiritual."[7]

---

6. Rieman, "Spirituality," 78.

7. *Catechism of the Catholic Church*, art. 362. Hereafter cited in parenthetical references as *CCC*, with article number.

Personal Experience

Experiences of the spirit or of life in the spirit are experiences of life in relationship. It is in the *cotidiano*, the day in and day out of relationships, that our spirit is lived, and it is in our actions that our spirit is manifested. Ultimately, if humans are spirit, then all human experience is somehow spiritual.

Spirituality is often described as life in the spirit. This description is fine; however it raises the question, "Which spirit?" Spirituality is an existential reality made up of the personal and communal experience of being moved by the human spirit, angelic or demonic spirits, team spirit, patriotic spirit, the spirit of this age, and/or the Holy Spirit, which is why there are so many spiritualities.

Paul coined the term "spiritual" to indicate the Christian as a person under the guidance of the Holy Spirit in contrast to the natural human being. However, since Vatican II we have discovered that just as there are Catholic, Protestant, Franciscan, Jesuit, clerical, and lay spiritualities (to name a few) there are also Jewish, Muslim, and Hindu spiritualities (to name a few). At the core of each type of spirituality is experience, both personal and communal.

Experience is also teaching us, Christians, that we have much in common with the spiritualities of many of the world's religions, especially in the desire for justice, peace, and liberation. Growing dialogue with the leaders of the various religions around the world helps us discover that we have much to learn from each other's spiritualities as well. Sadly, many Christians are also taking elements from other religions and spiritualities in ways that do not understand or respect the doctrines of those other faiths and using them to create a doctrine that lives merely to serve their individual needs.

Communal Traditions

At this point, for our purposes of explanation and because of my own experience, I will focus on Christian spirituality. At the heart of Christian spirituality is Jesus's personal experience of God as *Abba* and the mission that took him to the cross and beyond. But because Christianity became a communal spirituality, its heart also contains the experience of Jesus's disciples who came to see him as the Christ and risen Lord. Our Christian Tradition and traditions are born of this shared experience. So when we talk about Christian spirituality as life in the spirit, the spirit in question is our spirit led by and in relationship with the Spirit of Jesus within a Christian community.

Spirituality is necessarily a communal reality that deals with some type of religious/cultural tradition(s) and/or (saintly) heroes. A true Christian spirituality requires contextualization, which is to say, it happens in one's context, in one's *cotidiano* where our culture, religion, and personal experience meet. Today, spirituality is the common ground of the three basic components that make up tradition: culture, religion, and personal experience.

Academic Discipline

Spiritualogians speak of spirituality as a discipline that can be studied in an academic or scientific manner. Some call this academic discipline/science "spiritual theology," while others prefer to refer to it as "spirituality."

As any science, spiritual theology has an object and method of study.[8] It studies (1) the spiritual itinerary (path or journey) and its various phases, (2) the reality of the Christian spiritual life as a lived and historical phenomenon, and (3) the legitimacy of diverse Christian spiritualities—the significance of their variety, criteria for authenticity and discernment, their relationship with singular Christian spirituality. Primarily this is done using a theological method of speculative deduction from the principles upon which Christian life is based and lived.

According to Sandra Schneiders, "spirituality" is the most appropriate name for the emerging discipline for four reasons:

1. Like psychology, anthropology, sociology, and other human sciences, it needs to develop freely in terms of its proper subject matter and scholarly approaches.

2. This name helps avoid making the theological method its primary scholarly approach to the detriment of interdisciplinary contributions by other sciences, especially the human sciences.

3. It is a term that has only gained popular usage by non-Catholics in the last forty to fifty years, thus it does not carry the baggage that

---

8. Moioli, "Teologia spirituale," 1602, 1608.

the term *theology* does and can facilitate intercultural and inter-religious dialogue on the subject.

4. Unlike *mysticism*, *spirituality* denotes the living out of one's faith, religion, transcendence, and search for ultimate meaning in one's *cotidiano*.[9]

Spirituality is a self-implicating, and interdisciplinary endeavor that can utilize a variety of methods and other academic disciplines such as psychology, history, and theology for its study. As with any science, spirituality has a subject and a method, but the spiritualogian is intimately involved in the subject of study, that is to say in the spiritual life, the conscious attempt to integrate one's life through self-transcendence and striving towards the ultimate value/meaning of life.[10] For Christian spiritualogians this means studying life in the Spirit. Doing so will both comfort and challenge the scholar in his or her own personal life. This means that the method of spirituality is participative or self-implicating while at the same time seeks to appropriate what is learned for a more general audience than just one's self.[11]

Ultimately, like spiritual theology, Christian spirituality is interested in helping Christians grow in their spiritual life, which is to say, as Christians in every part of their *cotidiano* and not just the purely "religious." Christian spirituality is a holistic science touching every aspect of a person's life with the grace of the Spirit.

SPIRITUALITY AS AN ART

I confess that as a professor, I like talking about spirituality as a science and I expect my students to do critical work with visible methodology. But in my personal life I prefer to think of Christian spirituality as an art form. I admit that a historical perusal (no matter how short) of the term *spirituality* and consideration of the ontological, experiential, communal, and academic natures of the subject can suck the wind out of anyone's sails. The very words *scientific* and *academic* seem to cast the

9. Cf. Schneiders, "Spirituality in the Academy," 690–91.

10. Cf. Ibid., 678; Frohlich, "Spiritual Discipline," 65–78.

11. Depending on the spiritual classic being studied, spiritualogians use a variety of methods, which include hermeneutical method, theological method, historical method, anthropological method, and the appropriative method. Cf. Downey, *Understanding Christian Spirituality*, 123–31.

"Spirit" right out of spirituality. For this reason, I like the Italian theologian Giovanni Moioli's referring to the field of Christian spirituality as an art form.[12] Like all art forms, Christian spirituality takes practice and study, but essentially, it is a gift and a grace, which can be trained and developed like any artistic skill.

According to the ancient Toltecas[13] of Mexico, the true theologian is the artist. It is the artist who in painting, sculpture, poetry, song, and dance can explain God to the soul in ways theology cannot. A beautiful song, a graceful dance, a vibrant painting can lift the human spirit to the heavens higher than any doctrinal explanation, biblical exegesis or theological treatise. One does not become such an artist, however without talent. Talent cannot be learned. It is God given. It can, nonetheless, be sharpened and developed with years of study and practice.

Art is also a science and an academic field. In it students learn how to dissect, analyze, and investigate the work of other artists. They learn to look beyond the art piece, in order to see its design, balance, color scheme, composition, and subject in order to nurture and improve their own talent. One cannot be truly spiritual without the grace of the Holy Spirit. Furthermore, one becomes a spiritual giant or a wisdom figure only through study and practice in the art of spirituality, learning from the saints, masters of the past and the practitioners of the present. Still, all study and practice of spirituality is useless without inspiration. Inspiration, like its root word *spiritus*, blows where and when it will, until then the artist continues to study and practice techniques that will help to turn the winds of inspiration into a song, a whistle, a whisper, or a moan in the hearts of those who see her or his art.

IN CONCLUSION

Christian spirituality is a self-implicating art. As we read about it and study it, it challenges us and comforts us; it becomes socio-implicating and moves us beyond piety to life, to action, to liberating ourselves and others so that together we can transform the world.

12. Moioli, "Teologia spirituale," 1602.

13. The Toltecas or Toltecs were a Nahuatl tribe that lived in what is now Mexico City. They were eventually vanquished by the Aztecas. Their thought, religion, and poetry, however, were superior to that of the Aztecas, who chose to incorporate those things into their own civilization much like the Romans had done with the ancient Greek philosophies and art; cf. Ward, "From the 'People,'" 225–31.

In the following chapters, we will study the art of a liberating Christian spirituality by reflecting on its context, participants, content, processes, and aspirations in light of the peace, justice, and liberation orientation of the Gospel. In this manner we will answer the following questions:

- Where is spirituality lived out? (chapters 1 and 2: journey and reality)

- Who helps and challenges us to grow as Christians? (chapter 3: God's family)

- What informs our spiritual formation and growth? (chapter 4: God's Word)

- How do we express and strengthen our Christian spiritual life? (chapter 5: liberation)

- Why do we live it? What is our ultimate goal? (concluding chapter).

Answering these questions will give us a better appreciation for the art of Christian spirituality. It is a participative form of painting in which the artist brushes him/herself onto the living canvas that is a community's spiritual tradition and outreach. Each of us is charged with being such an artist.

DISCUSSING THE INTRODUCTION

Questions about the Material

What are the four categories of understanding used to discuss spirituality?

What is *cotidianidad* or *lo cotidiano*?

When and why was the word *spirituality* coined?

Questions about Your Own Experience

How do you define or describe spirituality?

What is your experience of Christian spirituality?

Does reading this material touch your spirituality in any way?

What does spirituality have to do with your call to be a Christian in the world?

1

The Spiritual Journey

IN A BEAUTIFUL POEM that is often read at Jewish funerals, Rabbi Alvin
Fine wrote, "life is a journey." He compares life to a "sacred pilgrimage"
that is "made stage by stage—from birth to death to life everlasting."[1] It
is growing . . .

> From childhood to maturity and youth to age;
> From innocence to awareness and ignorance to knowing;
> From foolishness to discretion and then perhaps to wisdom.[2]

Thanks to the liberating Exodus experience of ancient Israel, these concepts of pilgrimage and journey are very important to our Jewish brothers and sisters. They are also very much a part of the inheritance we
Christians have received from our Jewish founders. As itinerants (people
who travel from one place to another), Jesus and the early disciples experienced firsthand what it meant to journey through life. Therefore,
journey became an important symbol in Christianity.

Journey as a metaphor for life indicates the importance of movement and growth. Life is not static. It is full of change. It is progress,
development, and formation. In children, the realities of growth and
development are self-evident as their bodies stretch and get bigger and
their minds and hearts develop intellectually and emotionally. We have
only to look at a child mature from infant to teenager to realize that life
is made up of consecutive and intertwined stages. As we get older, the
reality of change gets less obvious, but no less real. Children and adoles-
cents are not the only ones who go through stages and transitions in life.
Adults move through stages of maturation to attain the wisdom of old
age. They also go through moments of crisis and change at the hand of

1. Fine, "Life Is a Journey."
2. Ibid.

varying circumstances found in the *cotidianidad* of life. And this is true not just of the individuals, but also of communities and institutions like the Church. The Church is now 2000 years old, and as such it has seen its share of changes and transitions as it grows in fidelity to Christ and the Gospel.

THE PILGRIM CHURCH

From 1962 to 1965, the bishops of the Catholic Church met in a synod that is known as the Second Vatican Ecumenical Council, or Vatican II. The council wrote a number of important documents, the first of which was the Dogmatic Constitution on the Church, *Lumen gentium* ("Light of the Nations": *LG*). In it, the bishops set the tone for the changes that were to come from Vatican II and defined the Church as a pilgrim people (see sidebar). Throughout the centuries, the Christian community has latched on to various symbols, typologies, and metaphors in order to explain who we are to others and to ourselves, to explain how we relate. We have called ourselves the followers of Christ, the mystical body of Christ, the Church militant, the house built on a rock, the bride of Christ, and mother of believers, to name a few. Since Vatican II we have taken to considering ourselves the pilgrim people of God. We are in the world but not of the world.

> ### PILGRIM CHURCH
>
> Priest and songwriter Cesáreo Gabaráin wrote a beautiful song entitled "Iglesia Peregrina" (Pilgrim Church), which sums up the spirit of Lumen gentium. He reminds us that, thanks to our common baptism, we walk through this world as the body of Christ guided by and filled with his Spirit. As we travel through this world we are the seeds of another kingdom, which is a reign of love, peace, and light.

To understand what we mean by this, we need to look at how Vatican II uses this image in *Lumen gentium* (*LG*). The term first appears in article 7 of the Constitution on the Church and focuses on the members of the Church being "molded in the likeness of Him, until Christ be formed in them." This being conformed to Jesus Christ occurs in our participating in his death and resurrection as we "are taken up into the mysteries of His life, until we will reign together with Him" (*LG* 7). This happens already at baptism where we symbolically die to our old selves in order to be born again in Christ (Rom 6:3–7). Moreover, it hopefully continues to live itself out as we grow in our Christian calling in the world around us.

Lumen gentium goes on to say, "On earth, still as pilgrims in a strange land, tracing in trial and in oppression the paths He trod, we are made one with His sufferings like the body is one with the Head, suffering with Him, that with Him we may be glorified" (*LG* 7). The pilgrimage of Christian life is one of being born again in Christ. Through the work of the bishops, Jesus "guides the People of the New Testament in their pilgrimage toward eternal happiness" (*LG* 21).

Expressing the reality of the Christian Church, *Lumen gentium* focuses on the Church on earth as being part of the Church in heaven in an incomplete, dynamic, "already but not yet" sort of way. In other words, we share on this earth a foretaste of heaven. The pilgrim Church on earth unites with all the faithful who have gone before her into glory (*LG* 50). For example, the saints in heaven have already lived their earthly pilgrimage and reached the end of the journey. They serve as examples of what the pilgrimage can entail and how it should be traveled. First among these examples is the Blessed Virgin Mary (María) who lived a pilgrimage of faith that brought her to union with her Son (*LG* 58). And she is not alone; people like Joseph, the apostles, Mary Magdalene, Augustine and Monica, Francis and Clare of Assisi, Juan Diego, Martín de Porres, Rosa de Lima, and Theresa of Calcutta have all been set up as examples of how the Christian pilgrimage is journeyed.

The journey of God's pilgrim people is one whereby the individual believer and the entire community of the faithful are being conformed to Christ. Unlike the pre-Vatican II Church, which stressed stability and structure, the pilgrim Church of Vatican II focuses on movement and growth. For example, the pilgrim Church looks for ways to adapt (inculturate) the Gospel to the many different cultures around the world. It seeks to grow in new ways of bringing the Good News to the world via mass media and new technologies. In all of this, the Church relies confidently on the Spirit of the Lord. The Church, as the People of God, is not only graced by the Holy Spirit, it is led by the Spirit of God as it moves in pilgrimage towards fuller union with God through conformity to Christ.

PILGRIMS AND STRANGERS

Christian history is a two-thousand-year pilgrimage filled with a variety of significant events and moments that help us define our identity as followers of Christ. In that journey, Vatican II was probably the most important event in the twentieth century for Church history. A renewed stress on the Sacred Scripture plus exposure to existential philosophies and other world religions during the first half of the twentieth century made the Church take a more serious look at itself.

Like every person who wants to grow and improve him or herself, the Church as a whole stopped and took a good look at ourselves. We discovered that we (not just the hierarchy) are the Church, and, as such, we truly are pilgrims and strangers in this world (cf. Heb 11:13; 1 Pet 1:11). To quote Jesus, our community is centered on a kingdom that "does not belong this world" (John 18:36); rather, ours is a people on pilgrimage *through* this world and so we are *inmigrantes* (immigrants) in a foreign land. Like all pilgrims, its members desire to reach a sacred place, which Jesus calls the Reign of God. And because we are all on this journey together, we can find ways to relate to one another both as spiritual beings and as human beings.

Take, for example the pilgrim's path that Arturo and I walked to Santiago de Compostela (see sidebar). Being a pilgrim on foot as a stranger in a foreign land gave me a unique insight into the language of the pilgrim people of God used by Vatican II. We are not tourists or wayfarers—we are pilgrims and strangers. We have a place to go, a destination in mind. We are not just in it for the adventure, although we should not shy away from learning from the adventure. We are not the only ones on the road, and cultural, religious, and language differ-

PILGRIMAGE TO SANTIAGO

A number of Catholic travel programs offer pilgrimages to the Holy Land, Rome, Lourdes, and many Christian shrines around the globe. These are great opportunities to connect with the Sacred in our lives. Sadly, these organized pilgrimages do not always give us the time to relish the pilgrim experience. Flying from one place on the planet to another and sitting in air-conditioned buses watching the locals and the countryside weaken the pilgrimage experience. Historically, pilgrimages happen on foot.

ences do not matter as long as we are on the road. What does matter is faith: faith in God, reliance on our fellow travelers, and trusting that the destination is worth the journey.

To be Christian is to walk in pilgrimage. It is to take Jesus seriously as the Alpha and the Omega, the beginning and the end of our journey. Jesus is the way, the truth, and the life (John 14:6). As pilgrims in faith, Jesus is the way we walk. In the journey, his attitudes slowly become our attitudes; his values our values. Jesus is the truth that frees us up to journey in community and reality. Jesus is the life in which we walk and the life toward which we are walking. He is the life that gives birth to our pilgrimage, to our journey, as we live out our earthly days en route to our eternal destination. And so, we live in the truth that if Jesus is our way then we are not only pilgrims on this earth, we are also strangers, *inmigrantes*. Our home is not of this earth, and so, like all human beings, we walk.

TO BE HUMAN IS TO WALK

The French philosopher, Christian existentialist, and playwright Gabriel Marcel (1889–1973)

(cont.)

Pilgrims in medieval Europe left behind well-worn pathways to Rome, Palestine, and northern Spain as they traveled to the tombs of the apostles in Rome, the holy shrines of Jesus's earthly life, and the tomb of St. James in Santiago de Compostela. I have had the opportunity to go to all three of the ancient pilgrimage centers. The journey to Santiago in Spain made the most lasting impression on me: I walked it!

Arturo, my novitiate classmate, had open-heart surgery in 1995. Thanks to God, it was a success. Almost a year after the surgery, he wanted to make part of the pilgrimage to Santiago in thanksgiving for his continued good health and to pray for vocations to Franciscan life.

It took Arturo and me five days of walking, praying, arguing, laughing, huffing and puffing to get to Santiago. Along the way, we followed the path that saints and sinners had trod for over a thousand years. The thought of this comforted me and spurred me on. Besides the memories of former pilgrims to carry us, there were the chance encounters with

(cont.)
other pilgrims on the journey. We ran into people from all over the world, who were walking to the same destination. Sometimes we shared a meal, prayed together, or simply smiled. National and language barriers did not detract us from building communion with our fellow pilgrims as we strengthened the bonds of our common Franciscan identity with each other.

coined the expression *Homo viator*[3] (the walking human) in response to the prominent concept of the human as *Homo sapiens* (the knowing human). Marcel preferred to focus our attention not on what or how we know, but on the growth and maturation of the human person; a development that happens in our *cotidiano*, especially in our everyday relationships. Marcel and other Christian scholars look at human life as a journey of growth and at humans as itinerant beings. In order to grow, people need to engage in a journey and be "awakened to reality"[4] within a community of believers. The community we travel with through life encourages us and often insists that we look seriously at ourselves, at who we really are and the reality of our *cotidiano*.

Humans are wayfarers by nature. To be human is to walk, but to be Christian is to walk as pilgrim and stranger in the world. Our attitude should not be that of tourists or travelers, but rather that of *inmigrantes* and foreigners who like Jesus walk *through* this earth as strangers. This attitude is not a comfortable one, and we need to keep in mind a few things to achieve and maintain it:

- Being a pilgrim and a stranger presupposes that we are not yet where we need to be.

- We are called to grow, develop, and progress in a Christo-centric personality, with Christ as the guiding force in our lives

- Christian life is not static and structured; rather it is movement and transformation.

3. Marcel, *Homo Viator*.
4. Ibid., 22.

- Christianity builds on the reality that humans are relational beings. We use our interpersonal relationships to grow as people and better grasp the concept of God.

- Our Sacred Scriptures highlight the importance of being on a journey.

Gabriel Marcel rightfully points out that to be human is to walk, it is to grow in self-awareness and grow through self-improvement. This is especially true in the Judeo-Christian tradition. Our Sacred Scriptures point this out quite clearly.

JOURNEY IMAGES IN THE HEBREW SCRIPTURES

To be a person of faith is to walk. Itinerancy is an important component of what it means to be a person of faith in the Sacred Scriptures. Ladders and stairways, crossing deserts and wastelands, climbing mountains and heights, traveling to shrines and sanctuaries—these are the varied ways in which the Scriptures tell us the life of faith is a life in pilgrimage. According to Cistercian monk and spiritual writer Richard Byrne (d. 1992), these journey images and metaphors provide the key "that interprets the most foundational dynamics and questions of human existence in light of the Christian message."[5] To better understand what these journey images mean to us in our *cotidianidad*, we must first comprehend how they relate to the Scriptures as a whole.

The first journey found in the Hebrew Scriptures is that of creation; a journey led by the Spirit of God hovering over the waters (Gen 1:2), bringing the cosmos out of chaos. The book of Genesis is filled with more human journeys, beginning with humanity's expulsion from the Garden of Eden. Some journeys are escapes like that of Cain, who was banished for killing his brother Abel (Gen 4:8–16), while others are voyages of faith like that of Noah, who spent over 150 days in a boat full of animals floating over the waters of the great flood that almost destroyed the earth (Gen 8:4). After these early journey images, the book of Genesis introduces us to Abraham and Sarah leaving their homeland in faith to a new land that God has promised as their inheritance (Gen 12; Heb 11:8–10). Abraham and Sarah's journeys have led their descendents to say of them, "Our parents were wondering Arameans," which is to say,

5. Byrne, "Journey," 565.

they were *inmigrantes* (cf. Deut 26:5). This saying is meant to remind the children of Abraham and Sarah that we are an immigrant people, and as such, we should be grateful to the God who has always cared for and protected us in all our journeys.

The children of Abraham and Sarah spent a great deal of time traveling, wandering about trying to make a life for themselves and their children. Victims of famine, they ended up in Egypt, and from there they fled in the great Exodus experience that is at the heart of the pilgrim people of God.

The liberating Exodus experience was Israel's reentry into the Promised Land, the "land flowing with milk and honey." Through Moses, God liberated them from slavery and oppression and led them to a place they could call home. In the process, a column of cloud led them by day and a column of fire by night, taking them from slavery to liberation. This powerful experience of liberation has left a deep and lasting impression in the Children of Israel. Over the centuries, the children of Abraham and Sarah have trusted that servants of God like Moses will liberate the people. Judges like Deborah (Judg 4:4–5), kings like David and Solomon, prophets like Elijah, Isaiah, and Hosea, as well as women like Esther are all examples of God's servants in the centuries-old task of liberation. Time and again, they liberated Israel from its enemies, and just as often they were called to liberate Israel from its own sins and failures before God.

In the path of liberation, God's servants never walk alone. God comes with us. The Exodus experience lasted for forty years, which is symbolic of a long time. It became a journey of revelation and purification, in which the people of Israel proved to be both holy and rebellious. God revealed himself as the Lord of life and covenant. Because of the fickle nature of humankind, God set down commandments to help the people live their newfound liberation. He gave them the Law, setting before us "life and prosperity, death and doom" (Deut 30:15). The choice is ours to make. As humans, we all walk. Will we walk in God's ways or will we walk away from God? Will our walk lead us home?

As humans we wander through life hoping to become settled in a place we can truly call home. The Hebrew Scriptures speak of the people of Israel as having begun as Semitic nomads looking for a place to call their own. Wandering from place to place, they settled in Palestine and eventually became the great kingdom of David and Solomon. Still throughout the Scriptures, judges, prophets, and valiant women kept calling the kings and the people to symbols of the way, the road, and the journey. In these three metaphors, they referred to liberation through a proper life, solid morality, and true religion. Isaiah reminded the people of his day and reminds us as well that God's ways are not our ways (55:8–9), and Micah (6:8) teaches us that proper life, solid morality, and true religion can be summed up by doing right, loving goodness, and walking humbly with God.

In the Hebrew Scriptures God sets the path of liberation before us, and in the Christian Scriptures Jesus shows us how to walk it. For Christians, Jesus is the servant of God par excellence who liberates all people from sin, enabling them to overturn its consequences.

JOURNEY IMAGES IN THE CHRISTIAN SCRIPTURES

Our Jewish ancestors walked all over the Middle East in their journey of faith and liberation. Jesus himself walked all over Palestine, and his original followers took the journey as far as Spain and India. You have only to look at the maps that can often be found in different translations of the New Testament to know that the concept of journey was very much a part of the early Church. The travels of Peter, Paul, Thomas, and other missionaries filled the early period. They all walked as pilgrims and strangers going from one city to the next, planting the seed of God's Reign, baptizing converts, establishing churches, and teaching them the Gospel.

The language of pilgrim and stranger is not one that Jesus used directly. He did, however, encourage his disciples to take nothing for the journey (Mark 6:8), and to pick up their cross and follow him (Mark 8:34). In his final words at the Last Supper, he painted a picture of the disciple as one who lives in this world but still is not of this world (John 17:16). Like the Son of Man who has nowhere to lay his head (Luke 9:58), the Christian is encouraged to leave behind her or his attachments to this age (cf. Luke 14:26–33; Matt 19:21–27). Oftentimes, our biggest attachment is to ourselves, to our way of thinking and our way of doing things. The pilgrimage I took with Arturo to Santiago de Compostela, for example, helped me to see that pilgrims need to travel light both literally and figuratively. Our backpacks and our hearts should be free of anything that is superfluous and would weigh us down and make both the physical and spiritual journey up and down mountains harder.

Let's consider some of the journey examples in the Scriptures. The Christian Scriptures begin using journey metaphors and images with the Virgin María. It all began with the Archangel Gabriel who traveled to Nazareth for the Annunciation. This journey from heaven to earth set María off on her own travels, first to Elizabeth's house, then to Bethlehem, her flight into Egypt, and finally back to Nazareth. When Jesus was twelve, she, Joseph, Jesus, and the rest of the clan went on pilgrimage to Jerusalem. It was during this pilgrimage that the child Jesus began to show signs of his future mission, of who he was becoming.

We know that Jesus returned to Galilee with María and Joseph, where his life continued in secret. These so-called hidden years of Jesus's life have inspired many to theorize that he must have traveled to India and other far-away places to get the knowledge he later teaches in Palestine. The truth is probably less exotic. His becoming the "Servant of God" took the commonplace journey of what we call *cotidianidad*.

We do not know what happened in Jesus's life from twelve to thirty years of age. We do know that during that time he was home in Galilee with María, growing in wisdom, stature, and grace (Luke 2:51–52). If Paul is right and Jesus became like all other humans (Phil 2:7), then his was the journey of *cotidianidad* we call growing up. He had to come to grips with his vocation in life and with whom God was calling him to become—the suffering Son of Man. We can all relate to the chaos and confusion that a human encounters when faced with the reality of whom s/he is called to be and whom s/he is called to be with. Normally, this happens at adolescence, which in U.S. and other Western cultures has extended itself into the late twenties and early thirties for many people. The hidden years of Jesus from twelve to thirty fit neatly into the extended adolescence of contemporary Western societies. Jesus's search for self-identity eventually took him to the river Jordan, where John baptized him. At that time, the Spirit of God pushed him out into the wilderness where Satan tempted and tested him. Likewise, I would venture to say that for most of us the journey of self-discovery is not an easy one. Our own lives are filled with temptations and tests that move us from one transition to another in our growth process and life journey.

JESUS'S SELF-EMPTYING JOURNEY

Jesus's journey is one of self-emptying, known as *kenosis* in Greek. *Kenosis* carries a connotation of abasement and humility. It appears in Paul's letter to the Philippians (2:6–11). In verse 7, Paul writes about Jesus's *kenosis* in amazement. In his Incarnation Jesus emptied himself, made himself nothing, humbled and abased himself. Through these acts,

Christ Jesus becomes one among the many, a nobody, taking on an unassuming nature. To Paul and to us, this *kenosis* of Jesus is even more incredible when we consider that he is God.

The mystery of the Incarnation is at the heart of Christianity and therefore the roadmap for the Christian pilgrimage. Paul and other New Testament writers witness to the kenotic journey of Jesus, the "Word made flesh," who "did not regard equality with God something to be grasped" (John 1:14; Phil 2:6).

The hymn in Paul's letter to the Philippians invites the reader to adopt the kenotic attitude of Christ (Phil 2:5–11; see sidebar). It calls us to embark on a journey where we follow the way of Jesus. In the Gospels, Jesus uses the invitation "Follow me" repeatedly. He invited Peter, Andrew, James, and John with "Follow me and I will make you fishers of people" (Matt 4:19). Kenotically they abandoned their nets and followed him. With a simple "Follow me," Jesus invited Matthew the tax collector and the rich young man. We know that Matthew accepted the invitation and the rich young man did not. The choice to follow is a free one and it sets us on a kenotic journey where we gradually adopt Jesus's way of thinking, feeling, and acting as part and parcel of our personal identity.

Philippians' Hymn

Scholars believe that Paul took the words of a hymn that was sung by Christians of his day and worked it into his letter to the Philippians. It expressed the teaching he was trying to convey to them and to us: we cannot be concerned with numero uno. Ours is a lifestyle based on the way of Jesus, which is the way of kenosis, humility, and service. In this way we work out our salvation (Phil 2:12):

Have among yourselves the same attitude that is also yours in Christ Jesus, Who, though he was in the form of God, did not regard equality with God something to be grasped. Rather, he emptied himself [kenosis], taking the form of a slave, coming in human likeness; and found human in appearance, he humbled himself, becoming obedient to death, even death on a cross. Because of this, God greatly exalted him and bestowed on him the name that is above every name, that at the name of Jesus every knee should bend, of those in heaven and on earth and under the earth, and every tongue confess that Jesus Christ is Lord, to the glory of God the Father. (Phil 2:6–11)

AN IDENTITY-BUILDING JOURNEY

In John's Gospel the invitation to follow Jesus becomes an imperative: "must follow me" (John 12:26). Those of us who have been baptized are called to continually remember our baptism by becoming more and more Christian, advancing in the life in the Spirit and growing in wisdom, age, and grace (Luke 2:52). I realize that if you are like most Christians you were baptized or somehow initiated into the faith as an infant. Like most of us, you did not have a choice. Somewhere along the way, I hope you have accepted the gift of baptism as your very own, not by being rebaptized but by living the commitment of baptism in your life. Every time you bless yourself with holy water or make the sign of the cross on your body, remember your baptism and live your commitment by rejecting sin by believing in Jesus Christ, and by loving and serving God and neighbor.

As Christians, we have been baptized in Christ and have put on Christ (Gal 3:27), meaning that we are called to think, feel, and love like Jesus. According to the baptismal ritual, we have died with him to one day be raised with him (Rom 6:3–5). But before this being raised with Christ can occur, we must walk/live in the "newness of life." We must give up the old ways of this world to live a new and improved life, a life of Christian charity and justice. In this way, we will be counted among the saints of God. We should not shy away from being a saint. Saints are not just special people who have been canonized as worthy of imitation. All the baptized are saints (we don't always act like saints, but we are all saints). Pope Pius XI reminds us, "All are called by God to a state of sanctity and all are obliged to *try* to attain it."[6] The Christian journey is a call to sanctity, by the God who makes us all saints.

The Christian journey begins with baptism and calls us into the work of identity building. This building is done by walking towards conformity with the image of God's Son, Jesus (Rom 8:29). Guided by the Holy Spirit, we figuratively walk towards the Father, becoming more and more like the Son in our pilgrimage. The walking is so important that we cannot stop along the way. Patristic writers "assert that we cannot remain stationary on the way that leads to God and to salvation."[7] As human beings, we "must pass from a beginning and through a middle

---

6. Pius XI, "Rerum omnium perturbationem," 27.

7. Tanquerey, *Spiritual Life*, 179.

course, a growth, and progression."[8] If we do not move forward, we move backwards. In other words, we must always continue to live in the way God hopes we can live; we keep moving forward and trying our best even in spite of the slips and falls along the way.

Christian identity building is a pathway filled with pitfalls, impediments, and hardship. In his classic *The Spiritual Life*, Adolphe Tanquerey invites us not to fear these obstacles, but "spurred on by the desire of advancing, we shall courageously resume our march, and our little setbacks, by exercising us in humility, will serve but to draw us nearer to God."[9] As a confessor, I have been privileged to be a part of people's drawing nearer to God. Often, I meet people who feel moved to come to confession after many years. When I ask them why, they confess that somehow God got through to them. Sometimes they return because they heard a good sermon or had a powerful religious experience. But often, it was because of some ordinary conversation with a friend, or an everyday experience that somehow opened their eyes to see that despite their various sins God loves them and calls them back.

The journey of becoming our true selves as images of God is not just about confronting our sins and limitations; it is also filled with beauty, wonder, and amazement. The beauty of a deep friendship, the wonder of nature, the amazement of feeling loved is all part and parcel of the Christian pilgrimage. Thank God, we do not travel it alone, but get to share the journey with others, our fellow saints. I cannot become a Christian without walking in and with a faith community (past and present). Our small successes will greatly encourage us as we move to the place where with Paul we can say: "I live, no longer I, but Christ lives in me" (Gal 2:20). The "Christian spiritual life is a progressive movement; a lifelong appropriation of salvation in Christ."[10] It is an embracing of our identity; we are all on the road to Christianity together.

BECOMING CHRISTIAN AS A LIFELONG PURSUIT

I say that we are on this road together because the road, the journey, the pilgrimage *is* the destination. Years ago, as a theology student, I had the opportunity to take a course from the Chilean theologian Segundo

---

8. Ireneaus of Lyons, *Adversus Haereses* 4.11, as quoted by Byrne, "Journey," 569.

9. Tanquerey, *Spiritual Life*, 213.

10. Byrne, "Journey," 569.

Galilea. I was struck by his insistence that we are not Christians. No one is! Rather, we are *becoming* Christians. Being Christian is not something static like being a finished clay jar. Earthen vessels like clay jars start by becoming, and in the hands of a skillful potter they eventually are what the potter wants them to be. Christians on the other hand never quite leave the potter's wheel. God's graceful hands are forever wetting, handling, and forming the clay. Likewise, we are continually embarking on our Christian journey.

To become Christian is to be a disciple, to follow Jesus Christ in the Church. The cross, conversion, confidence, conviction, commitment, community, and contemplation are all necessary conditions for this type of spiritual journey. Some of these are attitudes needed to make the journey and others are things to be encountered and embraced during the journey. You cannot become a Christian without the *Seven C's of the Christian Spiritual Life.*

The Seven Cs of the Christian Spiritual Journey

1. *Cross:* Christian spirituality begins with the cross; the cross of Jesus Christ, our own cross, and the crosses of our neighbors, especially the poor and marginalized. The cross is encountered and embraced as a paradoxical sign of salvation. That which often seems bitter and fatal can be sweetness and life.

2. *Conversion: Metanoia* in the Greek and *penitentia* in the Latin. Christians live lives of ongoing conversion meant to turn away from sin and death to embrace holiness and life. This demands faith and action.

3. *Confidence:* Christians need to trust confidently in themselves. They know they are loved and called by God who gives them what it takes to complete the journey.

4. *Conviction:* Trust in one's self is based on the conviction that God exists and acts in our lives. Christians are convinced that they will be saved in Christ and sanctified by the Holy Spirit.

5. *Commitment:* Christians are called to love God and neighbor by being dedicated to them in service. Commitment implies being bound to the other.

6. *Community:* Christians do not walk the way of Christ as solitary people. We walk together, building up a people of God that is formed of every race and tongue.

7. *Contemplation:* Ultimately Christians are called to contemplate God in all and to contemplate all with the eyes of God. That means seeing everyone and everything with the loving gaze of God.

A number of patristic writers remind us that becoming a Christian (progress in the Christian life) cannot happen without a beginning, middle and an end. In the works of Pseudo-Dionysius in the fifth century and St. Bonaventure in the thirteenth century, these three stages became the Triple or Threefold Way of Christian spiritual growth.

In his first letter John claims that Christians are children, youth, or parents in the faith (1 John 2:12–17). In this way he indicates a process of Christian maturation. During the patristic period (100–700 CE) a number of spiritual writers spoke of Christian maturation as three ages; beginners, adept, and perfect. These ages were also used in the language of apprenticeship. Master artisans had to go through three stages in the development of her/his craft. When they were first apprenticed to, let's say, a carpenter (Jesus was a carpenter), they were *beginners* who had to be taught how to handle the tools of the trade. The master carpenter plus the perfect would spend time with them teaching them how to hammer, saw, pick the right lumber, and other necessary skills. Eventually as they became more and more *adept* at their craft, they could be trusted to carry out small tasks on their own. Once they grew to *perfect* their craft, they could come up with their own designs and were able to execute them. They still, however, worked for someone else and were not considered master carpenters until they were out on their own and had apprentices of their own. How can we apply this to our Christian journey? Think of it like this: In Christianity Jesus is the only Master, so the perfect will always remain under his apprenticeship. We can (and need to), however, move from being beginners to becoming adept and hopefully perfect in the way of our Master. We are constantly studying in the way of Christ and learning new skills for living the life he had modeled for us to the fullest.

Pastoral theologian James Whitehead and his wife, developmental psychologist Evelyn Whitehead, replace the language of beginner, adept, and perfect with that of child, disciple, and steward in their work on

Christian maturation.[11] As previously mentioned, the need to work on our own Christian maturation, growth, or formation takes its cue in the New Testament (cf. 1 John 2:12–17; Heb; 5:12–14; Eph 4:11–15). Patristic writers like Clement of Alexandria, Origin, John Cassian, Evagrius Ponticus, and Augustine all added to the discussion of Christian maturation. But the training given to the apprentice Christians is not really defined until the fifth century. At that time, the mystic and theologian Pseudo-Dionysius tied the stages to three different wisdom books in the Sacred Scriptures. The beginners were encouraged to read the advice of the book of Proverbs, to help them along the Purgative way by teaching them how to embrace the cross, through a process of conversion and growth in confidence. For them Jesus was becoming the *way*. The adept were encouraged to read the ponderings of the book of Ecclesiastes as they progressed in the Illuminative way, strengthening their conviction and commitment to the Gospel way of life. They were being instructed in the *truth* of Jesus. Finally, the perfect were encouraged to read the Song of Songs so that in the Unitive way they could build up the community and enjoy perfect union with God through contemplation. In Jesus they had attained *life*.

In the thirteenth century another great mystical theologian, Bonaventure of Bagnoregio explained the Triple Way as the process by which we are purified and enlightened by God until we are able to be united perfectly to God. The three ways of purgation, illumination, and union, rather than being three ages of maturation or stages of growth, "constitute three efforts"[12] in the pilgrimage toward perfect union with God in Christ and through the Holy Spirit. According to Bonaventure, the three efforts help us to gain the peace of forgiveness, the truth of the Gospel, and the perfection of love. The three efforts teach us to follow Jesus as the way, the truth, and the life.

IN CONCLUSION

No one is born Christian, and even though we are baptized saints it takes a pilgrimage of faith to actually grow into our Christian identity and perfected sainthood. Along the way, we will be accompanied by a variety of beings, both human and divine. We will have to put into practice what

11. Whitehead and Whitehead, *Seasons of Strength.*
12. Cf. Z. Hayes, *Hidden Center,* 45.

we believe and reach out to those who are in need. But before considering who accompanies us and how we practice our faith we need to consider our reality as human beings. In the next chapter, I will invite you to embrace your reality.

DISCUSSING CHAPTER 1

Questions about the Material

What is *Lumen gentium*? How does it image the Church?

What are the seven "Cs" of the Christian spiritual journey?

What is *kenosis*? What does is have to do with Christian spiritual growth?

What are the three efforts of the Triple Way?

Questions about Your Own Experience

How do you describe your spiritual journey?

How do you feel about becoming a Christian?

What is your Christian calling in the world?

What is your experience of being a beginner (child), adept (disciple), and perfect (steward) in your Christian life or calling?

2

Embracing Our Reality

Having considered Christian life as a pilgrimage of faith, we now turn our attention to where that pilgrimage takes place, our *cotidianidad*, the reality of our day-to-day existence. Remembering the Central American martyr Ignacio Ellacuria (see sidebar), Latin American theologian Jon Sobrino explains that the key to understanding his profound faith was embracing reality. Ellacuria, like so many Christian martyrs and confessors, possessed "fidelity—to reality, to tradition, to faith, and finally to himself—he lived and remained attentive to a mystery, the mystery of God."[1] And even when embracing the harsh reality of the world we live in, Ignacio, like all Christian martyrs before him, knew that for Christians God is the ultimate reality. There is always more to reality than meets the eye.

Christians need to be guided by a spirituality that does not flee its reality, but rather embraces it as somehow part of God's Reign. Many people today have a dualistic view of spirituality that places it in competi-

IGNACIO ELLACURIA

The Jesuit philosopher and theologian Ignacio Ellacuria was one of over 70,000 people who died during El Salvador's 1980s civil war. He, five other Jesuits, and their housekeeper were killed on November 16, 1989, by the Salvadoran army on the campus of the Universidad Centroamericana "José Simeón Cañas" in San Salvador. His philosophy and theology focused on salvation as liberation from sin and all its consequences. He "said many times that the specifically Christian task is to fight to eradicate sin by bearing its burden. This sin brings death, but taking it own gives credibility."

1. Burke and Lassalle-Klein, *Love that Produces Hope*, 44.

tion or even enmity with material reality. Some Christians tend to see spirituality as something so transcendental that it is more other worldly than something of this physical world; more an interior truth than an external reality. This may be true of some types of spirituality, but not of Christian spirituality. Any spirituality that is worthy of the name of Christ needs to be a living, breathing, organic entity, like Christ himself. Jesus of Nazareth was not afraid of the real and material world. He met it head on. With his Incarnation and in his *cotidianidad*, he embraced the reality in which he found himself. In facing his temptations, healing the sick, welcoming the sinner, and accepting death he challenged its rough edges. We do the same when we struggle for justice, reach out to people in need, face our fears, and work to improve ourselves. Jesus also found in reality the hope of God's Reign, which is why he was able to use human relationships, natural cycles, yeast, pearls, lost coins, and other elements of daily life in his preaching. Again, we can emulate Jesus in this when we celebrate life, feel awe at nature, and appreciate the little things in life.

Jesus knew who he was. As son of María, he was a poor first-century Palestinian Jew living in a land that was occupied and dominated by Rome. This reality impacted his theology and spirituality. His message was deeply touched by his *cotidianidad* and the social, political, and religious context of his life. Embracing our reality begins with being aware of our identity and our context, in a word, our reality. Who we are and where we live will profoundly affect how we embrace reality. For this reason as Christians the first reality we need to embrace is ourselves as humans. In this chapter I will focus on the Christian understanding of human identity. I will then look at the importance of the Holy Spirit and what it means to embrace reality as Jesus did.

CHRISTIAN ANTHROPOLOGY: WHO AM I?

Our first reality is that of our human existence; it is who we really are as both humans and as God's creatures. For this reason it is important to stop now and consider who we are according to what we believe as Christians. While many people tend to regard spirituality as a set of practices and relegate it to a separate dimension of human experience, we need to understand that spirituality is "the way we relate to reality, confront reality, engage it."[2] Returning to the title of *Homo viator* from chapter 1, I need to add that more than being *Homo sapiens*, *Homo viator* is *Homo spiritualis*, which is to say, to be human is to be spiritual! As human beings, we cannot help but be spiritual. Spirit with a small *s* is one of the elements that make us who we are as humans and as individuals.

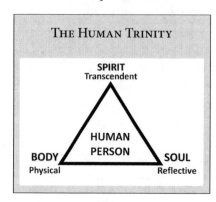

THE HUMAN TRINITY

SPIRIT
Transcendent

HUMAN
PERSON

BODY
Physical

SOUL
Reflective

Many Christians understand the human being as comprised of body and soul, but St. Paul in his letter to the Thessalonians indicates that the human person is a trinity of body, soul, and *spirit* (1 Thess 5:23/ CCC 367). If God is the Most Holy Trinity and we humans are created in God's image, then it makes sense that we are a trinity as well. Just as the Father (or Mother), Son, and Holy Spirit are One God, when we speak of body, soul, and spirit we are not talking about three separate elements. Rather, we are speaking of the physical, reflective, and transcendent dimensions of the one human person (see "The Human Trinity" sidebar). The physical dimension of our selves is our body

Often philosophers and other thinkers speak of the body as the home for our souls, but it is more than that; it is part and parcel of who we are—so much so that as Christians we believe that our body will rise again and be with us in heaven. So let's look at this marvelous creation that God has given us. It too is trinitarian. It is composed of genetics, environment, and exercise (or lack thereof). When we consider the reality of the human body, we discover that it is not one size fits all. Our body shapes, hair, and skin tones come in a wonderful diversity that only God can create. We are short and tall, thin and fat, dark and light, and bald and hairy, with every variation in between. The composition of our physical presence in this world is a product of our genes in combination with how we care for and exercise our bodies. Environment (where we live) can also greatly contribute to our bodies' health and well-being (or lack thereof) (see sidebar).

2. Ashley, "Mystery of God," 64–65.

The distinction between body and soul is palpable, but what is the difference between soul and spirit? Soul is usually seen as the center of human identity and being. The Latin word for soul is *anima*, from which comes the English word "animation." It is what animates the body and gives life and character to a person. It is what makes the person think, feel, and act/react. Basically, the soul is the cognitive, affective, and effective dimension of the person (see "Soul Dimensions" sidebar). It is hard to locate. Soul is often referred to as the mind, but in reality it is the brain, the heart, and the gut of a person. Traditionally the soul is where a person's intellect, emotions, and appetites are governed. Many Christian spiritual writers over the centuries have "taught that the original image of God found in the human person is, as "Augustine expressed it so vividly, revealed in the human heart, the intellect and the will."[3]

Whereas the body is the corporal/material dimension of the human person, the soul is the reflective dimension of the human being. Besides *anima*, the Latin word *mentis* is often used to refer to the soul, which may explain why it is often limited to the mind. Soul is all about intellect. It is about coming to know and understand life and reality, which is why it cannot be limited to mental

3. Hughes, *Spiritual Masters*, 36.

ENVIRONMENT AND THE BODY

I had the opportunity to experience firsthand how environment influences the body. In the 1990s I was sent to study and live in Rome with Franciscan friars from thirty-eight different countries. Over a period of seven years, I lived with about 210 friars. It was interesting to see how the brothers who came from developing nations tended to fatten up in Rome while at the same time those of us who came from the so-called First World countries tended to lose weight. Despite gelato and pasta, I managed to lose weight without dieting or even trying. The environment we live in can influence our eating and exercise habits, our breathing, our emotional state and other factors that contribute to how our body will be shaped, colored, and sculpted.

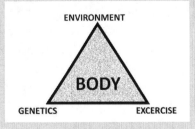

SOUL DIMENSIONS

The soul animates the human person and helps him/her grow in three ways:

1. *Cognitive:* the process of knowing and *think*ing as controlled by the intellect

2. *Affective:* the experience of *feel*ing as controlled by the emotions

3. *Effective:* the power of *action* as controlled by the appetites

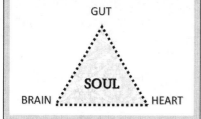

(rational) intelligence. It needs to be balanced with a physical (somatic) intelligence and an emotional (relational) intelligence. In many ways, rational intelligence can become a conduit or result of the interaction of physical and emotional intelligence. Somatic intelligence is closely tied to the body of a person; relational intelligence to a person's spirit.

Because of its rational, somatic, and relational nature, the soul is often referred to as the spiritual principle in humans (*CCC* 363). But where does that leave a person's spirit? If the soul enlivens the body and the eyes are the "mirror of the soul," it can be said that the spirit animates the soul, and one's reactions are the "mirror of the spirit." The Judeo-Christian tradition highlights the breath of God as what makes clay beings into human beings. The *ruah*, or spirit, is breathed by God into our nostrils and we become animate beings. Human experience suggests "we possess an innate spiritual impulse that lies deep in our human nature. This 'divine flame' is something we are born with, something that is essentially dynamic and forever seeking articulation and expression."[4]

All this is to say that at the core or *corazón* (heart) of the human person is the person's spirit, the person's desire to transcend him/herself in relationship with others and especially in relationship with the Totally Other, whom we Christians call God. I like to begin my courses and workshops on spirituality by having the students define spirituality. Strangely, they do not think to mention spirit, but more often than not they describe spirituality in terms of relationship. Humans are naturally relational creatures. It is here that we find the spirit, for relationship is all about self-transcendence in varying degrees, whether we are relat-

4. Schwartz, "Growing Spiritually," para. 9.

ing to others, to creation, or to God. Whereas the body and soul are the physical and reflective dimensions of the human person, the spirit is the transcendent/relational dimension of being human (see sidebar).

Fundamentally, human beings are spiritual beings. God is Creator, Redeemer, and Sanctifier; we are body, soul, and spirit. What we have in common with God is S/spirit. It is here that we are graced with God's presence, with the gift of life, with the desire to be whole, with the need for self-actualization, and with the nostalgic longing for love, happiness, and wholeness. We all have human spirit, which is why we can join St. Augustine in saying "Our hearts are restless until they rest in you [God]" (*Confessions* 1.1). In this way "spirituality is all about relationship, serenity, and purpose. It about those things all human beings aspire to in order to live an authentic human life. It is about the human spirit or the *corazón* being formed as it cries out for fullness and completion."[5] For Christians, the human spirit will only be fully realized when it works *en conjunto* (together/as an ensemble) with God's Holy Spirit.

HUMAN SPIRIT

According to Catholic teaching there is no duality in the human being. The human person is naturally made for transcendence, which is why s/he has not just a soul but also a spirit. The spirit raises the human being to the presence of God and is also the depths of being. It is what animates the person and brings her/him into relationship with others and the divine Other. Whereas the soul has often been associated with a person's mind, the spirit has been associated with the human heart, "in the biblical sense of the depths of one's being, where the person decides for or against God" (CCC 367–68).

THE SPIRIT OF GOD'S REIGN

Essential to embracing our reality is the acceptance of the Holy Spirit in the *corazón* and the lives of those who follow Jesus Christ as Lord and

---

5. Cavazos-González, "Cara y Corazón," 49.

Savior. The Hebrew and Christian Scriptures present the Spirit as the *ruah*, the *pneuma*, the breath that comes from God's mouth. As a result, besides having human spirit, all human beings have a shared interest in the Spirit of God, as a stockholder has shares in a company. Christians have a particular share in Christ. Thanks to Jesus, who pours out his Spirit on his faithful, we are temples of God's Holy Spirit and as such we are filled with the presence of the Most Holy Trinity in the core of our *corazón*, our spirit. The Spirit of God *en conjunto* with our spirit moves us to act as Christians in lives of prayer, devotion, ministry, and social action according to Catholic social teaching. To better understand this, let's take a look at a bit of history.

Catholic social teaching is said to begin with the work of Pope Leo XIII, who in 1891 wrote an encyclical on capital and labor entitled *Rerum novarum* (Of New Things). Six years later, this same pope wrote an encyclical on the Holy Spirit entitled *Divinum illud munus* (That Divine Office). With this encyclical of 1897, Pope Leo XIII became the first pope to attempt an explanation of the Holy Spirit. His work sparked a renewed interest in the Holy Spirit in Christian communities around the world. This new Pentecost eventually led up to the Second Vatican Council of the 1960s and to the charismatic renewal and liberation movements that came in the wake of that council. The charismatic movements and liberation theologies and ministry that burst onto the Catholic scene after Vatican II gave the Holy Spirit an importance almost without precedence in Western spirituality. Starting with the work of Pope Leo XIII, Christianity slowly discovered that adoration of God, social justice, and the Holy Spirit work hand in hand.

The Spirit, according to Pope Leo XIII, is the divine goodness and mutual love of the Father and the Son who gently and strongly completes and perfects the work of salvation begun by Jesus.[6] Our creed tells us that she is "the Lord and giver of life." The Spirit of God is recognized as the principle agent of liberation and human dignity, renewing individuals first and then the whole of society.[7] She is the one who spoke through the prophets against all forms of injustice. This same Spirit compelled Jesus to bring good news to the poor, to heal the sick, to liberate the captives and free the oppressed. The Spirit is the one who strengthens the

6. Leo XIII, *Divinum munus illud*, 3.

7. Cf. CELAM, *Puebla*, 203–4.

martyrs and inspires the Church to "historically incarnate life, on behalf of the poor"[8] in the reality in which it finds itself. The Spirit of God is the *corazón* of Christian spirituality.

Christian spirituality begins with a personal encounter with Jesus Christ, not as a historical/biblical character, but as a living and life-giving person who with his death and resurrection has achieved the liberation of humanity. For Christians animated by the generous Spirit of God, liberation is for and on behalf of others. In his encyclical *Spe salvi*, Pope Benedict XVI gives us the example of the African Saint Josephine Bakhita (see sidebar): "the liberation that she had received through her encounter with the God of Jesus Christ, she felt she had to extend . . . to the greatest possible number of people."[9] Christians must participate in the liberating mission of Jesus, who gave his life to liberate all people from sin and enable them to triumph over its consequences. In this manner we form a community of missionary disciples that walks together in the Spirit of Jesus.

Walking in the Spirit commits us to living a communal and committed life like Jesus did. Christian spirituality looks to the Son of God, who entered into human history in a very specific context, to learn

St. Josephine Bakhita

Born in 1868, this Sudanese woman was kidnapped at the age of seven and sold into slavery. She had several masters until she was finally sold to an Italian consul in Khartoum, Sudan. Two years later she was given to the Michieli family as nanny for their little girl.

She ended up in Venice with the daughter in a Canossian convent. While there she became a Christian. With the help of the sisters she refused to continue being a slave in the Michieli household. Her case went to the Italian courts that declared slavery illegal and therefore freed her.

She became a nun and spent the rest of her years in Venice and Verona serving her only master, Jesus Christ, in the poor who came to the convent looking for help or encouragement. She came to be known as "Madre Moretta" (dark skinned mother). In this way she lived in the Spirit of God's Reign and continued the liberating mission of Jesus.

8. Sobrino, *Liberación con Espíritu*, 13.

9. Benedict XVI, *Spe salvi*, 3.

(cont.)
She died in 1947 and was canonized in the year 2000. She is the patron saint of Sudan.

from him what needs to be done in our own various contexts. Jesus, the Son of María, presents himself as the faithful Child of the Father who in his mercy sends him to rescue and liberate the needy from the power of Satan and sin.[10] Following in his footprints, Christians must also rescue and liberate people who suffer the consequences of sin, especially social sin. African American preachers fighting the sin of racism in the last century taught us that the Spirit calls us to "a mirroring of Jesus' activity on behalf of the despised."[11] Jesus and his disciples are concerned with the whole person in the ministry of forgiving sinners, liberating the oppressed, and healing the sick. He does not separate the spirit from the soul or the body. Liberation "must encompass all aspects of our lives such as spiritual, intellectual, physical, economic, political, cultural, and social."[12]

For 2,000 years, Christians with their style of life have been and still are characterized by the desire to think and act like Christ. In other words, they are characterized by their following in the footprints of the Lord. It is in this way or *sequela* that Jesus liberates the believer, not for his/her personal satisfaction, but to share in Jesus's divine filiation[13] (see sidebar) and for the love and service of neighbor. This *sequela* becomes a socio-spiritual itinerary that takes into account the historical and social reality in which it finds itself. For us in the United States of America, it becomes a U.S. American *sequela* in contexts that are increasingly more secular and materialistic. Often,

Divine Filiation

Filiation is the condition of being the child or descendent of a particular parent. In the case of divine filiation we are sons and daughters of God by sharing in Jesus's role as Son of God. The fact that Christians are called to share in Christ's divinity is an ancient teaching of the Church (2 Pet 1:4), and according to John Paul II it is the essence of the Good News.

10. Cf. Spiteris, *Vita cristiana*, 151.

11. Pinn, "Jesus and Justice," para. 4.

12. Dube, "Who Do You Say that I Am?" 347–48.

13. John Paul II, *Crossing the Threshold of Hope*, 21.

rather than turning to the Gospel to help us decide how to live in this country, Christians are turning to mass media and public opinion. Yet, our U.S. American *sequela* needs to embrace both the Gospel and our U.S. contexts by finding in them the action of God. In this way we can collaborate with the reality of the Reign of God that is growing in the world even in our moment in history. For example, one of the U.S. contexts that Christians need to deal with is the reality of immigration and the growing Latina/o presence in the Catholic Church. As Christians we cannot simply leave the plight of the immigrant in the hands of politicians. Our Christian spirituality calls us to embrace our historical context of the world around us and be welcoming to the immigrant.

SPIRITUALITY AND HISTORICAL CONTEXT

Embracing our own reality as human beings, as Spirit-filled and as contextual beings, is the foundation of any liberating spirituality. Because of this we need to be keenly aware of the historical context in which we find ourselves as Christians. Like Jesus, Christians have to live within a historical reality that will shape their participation in God's mission of bringing all creation to fullness of life. Virgilio Elizondo, the father of U.S. Latino/a theology, invites us to consider "that we will never truly appreciate the full meaning and significance of Jesus as savior and liberator unless we are keenly aware of our own historical and existential situation."[14]

Spirituality comes from our *encuentro* (encounter) with the historical Jesus who is also the Christ of faith. That encounter floods our historical reality with the Spirit of Jesus. It is from this Cristocentrism that a liberating spirituality develops. This Christocentrism "is not about a 'return to Jesus', but rather an authentic 'rescue of Jesus.'"[15] who has often been ignored or misunderstood by the Church in its various historical and cultural contexts. This means looking at Jesus in his historical context as a poor Jewish carpenter living in Roman occupied territory. His message and his deeds were naturally affected by his reality.

A liberating spirituality understands the "historical Jesus" in and through the complete history of Jesus Christ. He identified himself with the historical and social context in which he became incarnate. Jesus of Nazareth was motivated by a true respect for the reality that manifested

14. Elizondo, *Galilean Journey,* 1.

15. Cf. Casaldáliga y Vigil, *Espiritualidad de la liberación,* 115–21.

itself in the *cotidianidad* of the persons with whom he lived, and to whom he proclaimed the gospel of God's love for the world (John 3:16–17). He felt compassion for the multitude afflicted by Roman tyranny and by the weight of the Law. He acted on their behalf and stretched out his hand to liberate them, whether or not it was "socially acceptable." Despite the Sabbath laws, Jesus still healed the sick on Saturdays. Despite the prejudice against non-Jews, Jesus reached out to the Samaritan woman (John 4:3–42), Syrophoenician woman (Mark 7:25–30), and even the Roman centurion (Matt 8:5–13). Despite the people's disdain of certain types of people, Jesus ate and drank with tax collectors, women of ill repute, and other public sinners. Jesus knew the laws of his religion, the rules of his culture, and the imposition of foreign domination of his historical context.

History is the place in which the Spirit of the Lord incarnates Christian spirituality. Many spiritual writers reflecting on historical real-ity affirm that the Spirit acts in history through the poor. To this day, the poor Francis of Assisi is remembered by all kinds of people, while the powerful Pope Innocent III is known mainly to Church historians. This does not mean the Spirit of God has not acted in the power of the popes and emperors. The Spirit has done so, but still, it is interesting to note that during the period of greatest conflict between ecclesiastical and secular powers (twelfth and thirteenth centuries) the Holy Spirit mani-fested itself in poverty movements like the Franciscans, Dominicans, Augustinians, and others that challenged and renewed the Christian community in its social and historical reality.

"Fidelity to reality embraces the concrete socio-political, religious and economic conditions of a people in order to celebrate and enhance the positive elements of their lives. It also challenges anything in their world that promotes or is victimized by a 'culture of death."[16] Jesus proclaimed the coming Reign of God with his whole being; good news for the poor and marginalized; bad news for the rich and powerful. He saw the seeds of God's Reign in his context and at the same time he condemned those things that rejected God's Reign. He took ordinary things like the finding of a lost coin or the mercy of a loving father and used them to speak of God's Reign. He also condemned the legalistic approach to God's Law as contrary to God's Reign. As the servant of God, He gave his life in the struggle against sin. In that struggle he found "the need to carry that sin,"[17]

16. Cavazos-González, "Five Pillars," 84.

17. Sobrino, *Liberación con Espíritu*, 28.

letting himself be destroyed by "the tragic surprise of reality"[18] that not everyone desires or accepts the liberation offered by God.

IN CONCLUSION

Professor of Mission and Culture Stephen Bevans invites us to embrace our context by discovering that the "ordinary things of life are so transparent of God's presence, one can speak of culture, human experience, and events in history—of contexts—as truly sacramental and so revelatory [of God's presence]."[19] Embracing that reality is accepting that one will find both the positive and negative in it. Society today is often bound up in the chains of consumerism, power, and control, and yet it is filled with people who are free to be generous, act kindly, and struggle for justice and human dignity on behalf of everyone. Sin and grace abound in secular society, just as grace and sin are found in Christian souls. This is our contextual reality, and we embrace it by animating the positive and disabling the negative.

We cannot, however, embrace reality by ourselves; it is much too big. We embrace reality as members of God's household, which is to say, God's *familia*. In our next chapter we will consider various members of that *familia* and how they participate in a liberating spirituality.

DISCUSSING CHAPTER 2

Questions about the Material

What does reality have to do with Christian spirituality?

What is *Homo spiritualis*?

What is the trinity that makes up the human person?

How was Jesus faithful to reality?

18. Ibid.
19. Bevans, *Models of Contextual Theology,* 12–13.

Questions about Your Own Experience

Where are you living your Christian calling in the world?

Do you experience yourself as physical, reflective, and transcendent?

What does divine filiation mean for your life?

How are you faithful to reality in general?

How are you faithful to the reality in which you find yourself?

3

God's Liberating Family

IN THE 1990s I got my license and Doctorate in Spirituality from the Pontifical University of St. Anthony in Rome. As part of my studies I chose to write a thesis on St. Clare and the process for her canonization. I read and reread the official process of her canonization in Spanish, Italian, French, and English, but I could not settle on a topic that interested me. In speaking with my advisor he asked me if I had read the *Process* in its original language (thirteenth-century Umbrian). I told him I had not because I did not know medieval Umbrian. "No excuses" was his response, and so I read and reread the document in its original language. Eventually, I realized that it was a lot like my native-tongue Tex-Mex or Espanglish, in that it mixed languages along with their grammar and syntax. Medieval Umbrian, I discovered, was a strange mixture of Latin, Italian, and Spanish.

Once my eyes were opened, I discovered the word *liberation* and its verb forms all over the *Process*. The witnesses that testified on behalf of Clare's sanctity spoke of her as a liberator who performed works of liberation often and on a regular basis. Her spiritual journey was dedicated to the liberation that Christ offers to the human person: liberation from sin, from illness, from marginalization, from oppression, and from social woes. In her ministry of liberation, Clare, like Francis of Assisi, often called on the help of God and his family. She saw herself as a part of that family. She described that family as being made up of God, the Virgin María, Michael the Archangel, St. Agnes the martyr, St. Francis, and all the male and female saints. To these she added the male and female founders of religious communities, the hierarchy, the sisters, and all those who wanted to live a Christian life. Clare discovered that the Christian gospel of liberation is never lived alone.

Having looked into the reality of our human personhood, we will now consider the reality of those around us who make up the *familia* we belong to as Christians. Christianity, as Clare and all Christian saints discovered, is meant to be a socio-centered religion. Liberation is achieved by breaking with the ego-centrism of individualism. Christian spirituality happens in several relationships. No one grows or lives alone.

As the Renaissance poet John Dunne put it so eloquently: "No man [sic] is an island entire of itself; every man [sic] is a piece of the continent, a part of the main."[1] If this is true of all humans, it is especially true of Christians. No disciple of Christ grows or lives alone. The journey of spiritual growth and maturation is best walked in good company. This chapter will take into account the participants of our spiritual journey in light of liberation and justice: the triune God and the communion of saints. We will look at the three persons of the one God and then consider the communion of saints as made up of María, the saints and the Church. These are the people who help us grow as social-justice oriented Christians.

WE BELIEVE IN GOD

Sunday after Sunday, Catholics and other mainline Christians proclaim their profession of faith using one of the two creeds that come down to us from the apostles through the Council of Nicea in the year 325. The Apostle's Creed and the Nicene Creed have been the primary symbols of our faith as well as the foundation of our Catechism. The most recent version of the *Catechism of the Catholic Church* (*CCC*) follows a long tradition of Church teaching which seeks to explain what we believe. The Catechism begins with an explanation of the "object of faith," God, as defined in the Apostle's Creed. This explanation opens by stating "'I believe in God': this first affirmation of the Apostles' Creed is also the most fundamental. The whole Creed speaks of God, and when it also speaks of man [sic] and of the world it does so in relation to God" (*CCC* 199).

The Christian statement "I believe in God" affirms the Jewish prayer "Hear, O Israel! The LORD is our God, the LORD alone!" (Deut 6:4). However, in the Nicene Creed, the statement "I believe in God" does not stop there. It continues to affirm belief in the "Father, the Almighty" (see sidebar), "one Lord, Jesus Christ, the only Son of God" and the "Holy Spirit, the Lord, the giver of life." As the Catechism reminds us

---

1. Dunne, "Meditation XVII."

"Christians are baptized in the name of the Father and of the Son and of the Holy Spirit: not in the *names*, for there is only one God, the almighty Father, his only Son and the Holy Spirit: the Most Holy Trinity" (*CCC* 233). God has an inherent diversity in his oneness. This may explain why "God willed the diversity of his creatures and their own particular goodness, their interdependence and their order" (*CCC* 353). Diversity can be a symbol of God.

In her presidential address to the Academy of Catholic Hispanic Theologians of the United States (ACHTUS 2008), Latina theologian Carmen Nanko-Fernández spoke of human diversity and otherness as found "within the very being of God. In other words, God is like me, and God is not like me, God is like you and not like you."[2] In this way she addressed the inherent diversity of the human race and the two traditional approaches to God: the *kataphatic* and the *apophatic* (see table below). In other words God is like us and yet God is not like us. Or better yet, we are the image and likeness of God but God is totally other. The kataphatic approach to God relies on God's self-revelation in us and in everything around us, while the apophatic approach accepts the fact that we simply cannot say anything about God with any certainty. As Christians we believe that the God and Father of our Lord Jesus Christ is somehow both close (imminent) and distant (transcendent) at the same time. God is complete and total mystery and yet God is love.

> ## GOD: OUR MOTHER AND FATHER
>
> "By calling God "Father," the language of faith indicates two main things: that God is the first origin of everything and transcendent authority; and that he is at the same time goodness and loving care for all his children. God's parental tenderness can also be expressed by the image of motherhood, which emphasizes God's immanence, the intimacy between Creator and creature. The language of faith thus draws on the human experience of parents, who are in a way the first representatives of God. . . . God transcends the human distinction between the sexes. He is neither man nor woman: he is God. He also transcends human fatherhood and motherhood, although he is their origin and standard." (CCC 239)

2. Nanko-Fernández, "Theologizing en Espanglish," para. 12.

Traditional Christian Approaches to God

Imminent	*Transcendent*
Present in all things	Beyond everything
At the core of everything	Not like anything we know
Self-revelatory	Totally other
Approachable	Ungraspable
God is Love	God is Mystery
Kataphatic	*Apophatic*

Traditionally Western Christians have been very kataphatic or positive in our approach to God. God made us in God's own image and likeness and so we can learn about God by observing humans at their best. We humans can be very loving, caring, nurturing, and sacrificing; what does this say about God? We can be attracted to goodness, beauty, unity, and truth; again what does this say about God? At the same time humans can be weak, limited, sinful, and horrible beings; does this say anything about God?

Human beings are not God; we are images and likenesses of God, and therefore we cannot measure God by our standards and limitations. God may be imminent and close at hand, but ultimately God is transcendent and apophatic, which is to say, beyond all understanding. We will never be able to get a hold of God or to wrap our minds around him or her. God is neither male nor female and yet both. The apophatic or negative approach to God "invites us to transcend the limitations of creaturely experience and human thought. . . . it is safer to say what God is not than to try to assert what he is."[3]

I will admit, as both Latino and a Christian I find apophatic talk about God to be frustrating (see sidebar). It isn't called the negative way without a

> ### NEGATIVE (APOPHATIC) THEOLOGY
>
> There is nothing negative about negative theology. It is called that because it is an approach to God that focuses on the inadequacy of human beings to talk about God. Almost everything we can say about God can be negated, not because it is not true, but because God is so much more than human concepts or understandings can explain.
>
> Negative theology can be very positive because rather than try to explain God it invites the believer to stop thinking and simply experience God.

3. Payton, *Light from the Christian East*, 76.

reason. Our belief that God became a Jewish carpenter from Nazareth makes it hard for Christians to be completely apophatic. We like to talk about God. We believe that God has revealed God's self to us in the Jewish Law and the Prophets and then most especially in Jesus the Christ. We imagine God as one of us and speak of him with metaphors that come from very heart of human relationships. Our Jewish and Muslim brothers and sisters, however, remind us that God cannot be imaged. They have particular "concern not to associate anything or anyone with the one true God."[4] They are right; there is a lot that we cannot say about God. Still, one thing Jews and Christians and Muslims can say for certain is that God accompanies us. According to the Hebrew, Christian, and Muslim Scriptures, God is our *compañero*, which depending on our tradition can be imaged as companion, lord, parent, lover, spouse, or friend.[5]

We call God by diverse titles, knowing full well that none of those titles truly fits God, not even the title "God." Still, in our human limitation titles and images for God are all we have to describe and define the experience of the One we call God. This experience is a human experience, it knows no boundaries. God is experienced by both men and women; Christians, Jews, Muslims, Buddhists, atheists, and others; black people, brown people, white people, and all peoples; rich, poor, and middle class—in other words, the whole diverse human race experiences God one way or another, whether they know it or not.

WE BELIEVE IN JESUS CHRIST

In 1976 Pope Benedict XVI (then German theologian Joseph Ratzinger) published *The God of Jesus Christ*, a book on the Christian understanding of God. In it he describes God as "the act of seeing."[6] Basing his observation on Psalm 139, he claims that God knows humans and has accompanied humanity over the centuries. God is the *compañero* who also hears "the cry of the poor" and his people's suffering (Exod 3:7). Because God

4. Scott Alexander (Director of Catholic-Muslim Studies at Catholic Theological Union), in an e-mail message to author, June 16, 2009.

5. Scott Alexander explains: "The Quran and Islamic tradition refers to God as: 'Rabb al-'Alamin' (lit. the 'Nurturing Sustainer of the Universe'); as that One Being whose essence is compassion (al-Rahman) and who offers compassion to all of creation (al-Rahim); as the 'Lover' of all creation (al-Wadud); and as the 'Protecting Friend' of the faithful (al-Wali)—among other epithets denoting God's loving concern for human beings" (e-mail message to author, June 16, 2009).

6. Ratzinger, *God of Jesus Christ*, 18.

sees and hears, God is also a protector. The God of Israel, Jesus's *Abba*, "protects the rights of the powerless against the mighty."[7] In Jesus, the God who sees, hears, and protects also identifies with humanity, and as a result serious "consideration must be given to the manifold human experiences that mediate God's self-disclosure."[8] In Jesus, God "took on the defenselessness of one who was accused and condemned and died."[9]

Latino theologian Miguel Diaz (now U.S. ambassador to the Vatican) compares the entry of the second person of God into the human situation as a border crossing. "God's border crossing entails God's journey into a particular human landscape. The journey into a particular landscape precipitates God's both/and ways of being in the world. In Jesus Christ, God can be identified as being both human and divine. In Jesus Christ, God assumes a cross-cultural face."[10] The human experience of this divine *inmigrante* was one of lowliness, poverty, marginalization, and even victimization. In all this he experienced God as *Abba*, Lord, the woman with the lost coin, the father of the prodigal son, the one who seemed to abandon him on the cross, and the one who ultimately raised him up on the third day. His human experience legitimizes the human experiences of God.

A Christian spirituality that is liberating will take the diverse experiences of God into account, but most especially it will favor the experiences of the poor and the marginalized with whom Jesus so identified himself. In all four of the Gospels we find that Jesus chose to refer to himself not as the "Son of God," but the "Son of Man." This curious title is found in the Books of Ezekiel and Daniel. In Ezekiel God uses it to call the prophet, reminding him he is a mere mortal. In Daniel it seems to refer to the whole people of Israel who are suffering at the hands of the gentiles.[11] The Son of Man appears triumphant in a vision, coming to rule the world in God's name. The suffering Son of Man becomes the glorious Son of Man who is avenged by God and given power over his oppressors. It is no wonder that in Luke's Gospel (6:20–26) for every beatitude on behalf of the poor and the suffering Jesus adds a woe to the rich and the comfortable. To the poor and suffering, God is revealed

---

7. Ibid., 20.

8. Diaz, "Life-Giving Migrations," para. 2.

9. Ratzinger, *God of Jesus Christ*, 20.

10. Diaz, "Life-Giving Migrations," para. 24.

11. Cf. Browning, "Son of Man," para. 1; Walck, "Son of Man," 310, 319.

in Christ as one who "reflects human weakness and vulnerability but also requires human solidarity in suffering. . . . Jesus accompanies them in their lives and inspires them to accompany him in his suffering and death, his resurrection and exaltation."[12]

In Jesus, God once again reveals himself as *compañero,* one who completely identifies with humanity, with the poor and marginalized. Lest you think Jesus does not care for the rich and the powerful, I need to stress that Jesus's preferential option for the poor is not at the expense of the rich. Jesus may not have identified with the rich and powerful, but he did invite them and everyone to identify with him, to accompany him, to take up his yoke, to bear his cross, saying, "Amen, I say to you, whatever you did for one of these least brothers [and sisters] of mine, you did for me" (Matt 25:40).

WE BELIEVE IN THE HOLY SPIRIT

As *compañero,* the Lord Jesus, Son of God and Son of Man, chose not to leave us orphans upon his return to the right hand of the Father. He sent us another advocate, comforter, *compañero*: the Holy Spirit. From the moment of his own baptism in the river Jordan, the whole of Jesus's ministry had been Spirit-led and to the glory of the Father. Despite the very real threat of the cross, Jesus remained undeterred in his liberating mission of salvation. "Jesus' undeterred Spirit-led migration to the human injustice of the cross manifests the mystery of God's abiding presence on the margin of human history. From this margin, God rejects all margins."[13]

This "abiding presence of God on the margins" is the gift of the Holy Spirit, the Mother of the poor. While it is true that the presence and power of the Holy Spirit enlivens the Church and its worship, we cannot believe that the Spirit is given only for prayer and praise. "It is important to see the active presence of the Holy Spirit of Christ, not only in the sacraments, but also in our striving for righteousness, human dignity, and liberation from every form of oppression."[14]

The Sequence prayed on Pentecost Sunday (see sidebar) reminds us of the many things that we Christians rely on the Spirit for. The Spirit of God is recognized as the one who endows the faithful with seven sacred

12. Ruiz, *Mozarabs,* 179.

13. Diaz, "Life-Giving Migrations," para. 29.

14. Ciobotea, "Salvation," 823.

gifts. These are wisdom, understanding, counsel, fortitude, knowledge, piety, and fear of the Lord (Isa 11:1–3). "They make the faithful docile in readily obeying divine inspirations" (*CCC* 1831).

The Spirit is our comforter and our rest, but only if we labor hard. Besides the gifts of the Spirit, those who labor in the Spirit also bear the fruits of the Spirit: charity, joy, peace, patience, kindness, goodness, generosity, gentleness, faithfulness, modesty, self-control, chastity (Gal 5:22–23).

The gifts and the fruits of the Spirit are for the building up of God's Reign. It was the Spirit that compelled Jesus and took him out into the desert and then brought him back preaching the Reign of God. It is that same Spirit that Jesus breathed onto the disciples. That same Spirit as Mother of the poor has blown into the hearts of the faithful, sending the Church to care for her children through acts of mercy, charity, and justice. Like Jesus, the faithful person will be a Spirit-led person proclaiming God's Reign in word and deed.

As a Spirit-led person, the Christian is *compañero* or *compañera*, friend, disciple, lover and spouse, son or daughter, brother or sister of God the Father/Mother, Son, and Holy Spirit. In this way s/he enters into the *familia* of God. But a relationship with God needs to be a nonexclusive one. The

---

PENTECOST SUNDAY SEQUENCE

Come, Holy Spirit,
And from heaven send forth
The rays of your light.

Come, Father [Mother] of the poor;
Come, giver of gifts,
Come, light of our hearts.

Most excellent Comforter,
Sweet guest of the soul,
Sweet cool refreshment.

Rest in our labor,
Restraint in the heat of desire,
Solace in our tears.

O Light most blest,
Replenish the innermost heart
Of your faithful.

Without your divine will,
Nothing is in a person,
Nothing is innocent.

Wash that which is sordid,
Irrigate that which is dry,
Heal that which is wounded.

Bend that which is rigid,
Warm that which is cold,
Straighten out that which is crooked.

Endow your faithful,
Who confide in you,
Seven sacred gifts.

Give us the merit of virtue,
Give us the success of salvation,
Give us perpetual joy.
Amen. Alleluia.

Christian is part of a traditional *familia*, in other words, it is an extended family made up of a communion of saints that includes María, the saints, and the Church. The rest of this chapter will look at all three. Let's begin with María.

BORN OF THE VIRGIN MARY

First among the disciples of Jesus and in the communion of saints is the woman from Nazareth that we know as María or Mary. As a child this young woman from an insignificant village in first-century Palestine could not have known just how important she would become to people all over the world. Her parents named her Miriam, but today there are so many titles for her that it is hard to settle on just one. But who says we have to settle on just one? Whether you refer to her as María, Mary, Mother of God, Guadalupe, Lourdes, Fatima, Madonna (to name a few), you are still speaking of the one and only Miriam of Nazareth, mother of Jesus. But where do all these titles and names for her come from. Like her son, Jesus, Mary is known by a variety of names and titles. Many of these are based on the Bible, dogmas (Church teaching), devotional practices, shrine locations, or are explanations of her role in the plan of salvation. Here is a sample list by category.

Marian Titles

Biblical
Full of Grace
Mother of the Lord
Virgin
Our Lady of the Visitation
Intercessor (at Cana)
Woman
Woman Clothed in the Sun

Dogmatic
Theotokos
Mother of God
Immaculate Conception
Ever Virgin
Assumption

Locations
Santa María del Pilar
Saint Mary of the Angels
Santa María de Guadalupe
Our Lady of Fatima
Our Lady of Lourdes
Our Lady of Częstochowa
Virgen de San Juan de los Lagos
Our Lady of Knock
Nuestra Señora de la Caridad del Cobre
Our Lady of Montserrat
Nuestra Señora de Corromoto
Nuestra Señora de Chuiquinquirá
Our Lady of Ngome
Our Lady of La Vang
Notre Dame du Cape

Devotional	Explanatory
Saint Mary	Tabernacle
Blessed Virgin	Seat of Wisdom
Madonna	Spouse of the Holy Spirit
Our Lady	Mother of Jesus
Notre Dame	Daughter of the Father
Blessed Virgin	Daughter of Zion
Queen of Heaven	Mother of the Church
Our Lady of the Rosary	Help of Christians
Our Lady of the Scapular	Mother of Grace
Our Lady of Sorrows	Ark of the Covenant
Immaculate Heart	Throne of Grace
Black Madonna	Spiritual Vessel
Prompt Succor	New Eve
Santa María del Camino	Sublime Example
Our Lady of the Miraculous Medal	Sister in Faith

The Gospels give us differing images of this young woman who gave birth to God's Son, the Messiah. The oldest Gospel, Mark, recalls her failed attempt at seeing Jesus (Mark 3:31–35) and only gives us her name three chapters late in Mark 6:3. He calls her *Mariam*, the Greek translation of the Hebrew name *Miriam*, which means "rebellious." *Miriam* can also be translated as "bitter water" and "drop of the sea."[15] In any case, it seems that she was named after the Hebrew prophetess and sister of the great liberator of Israel, Moses.

As we continue looking at the Gospels we find that Matthew speaks of her as a young Jewish woman who gets pregnant without explanation. When her mysterious pregnancy is finally explained, it is to Joseph and not to her. In this way, Matthew stereotypically depicts Maria as most women of her time, subservient to her husband and unable to truly understand religious matters. Mark and Matthew's image of Mary is not the María we are used to. But at least they give us a bit more information than Paul does in his letter. He only mentions her in passing (Gal 4:4).

The María most Christians are familiar with is found in the Gospels of John and Luke. John is the last of the four Gospels to be written, but strangely John's Gospel never mentions Jesus's mother by name. Nonetheless, John shares with us two of the most beloved stories of María in Christian memory: that of the wedding at Cana and the foot

15. Schmiedel, "Mary," 2953; Campbell, "Mary."

of the cross. For John, María is Ecclesio-typical: she is more than simply Jesus's mother, she is the Church.[16] María is Jesus's disciple. At Cana she is an intercessor, and on Calvary she is mother and model of all disciples.

As mother and model of Jesus's disciples, María is in John's Gospel a symbol of the Church; the Church that stands at the foot of the cross with all the suffering people of the world and the Church that intercedes on behalf of the needy as at Cana. "Mary displayed Christian love by helping the poor couple on their wedding day, especially in asking Christ for help. . . . she has great sympathy with the poor couple and did not think it beneath her to help them."[17]

In speaking of the events at Cana, Church historian Beth Kreitzer ascertains that "perhaps Mary was *too* zealous in her loving concern, as Christ's harsh response to her might indicate—it pushed her to interfere with his plans."[18] Over the centuries, Mariology (see sidebar) has shown that besides being Ecclesio-typical, María is also Christo-typical, she has a part to play in the plan of salvation that is carried out in Christ.

> **MARIOLOGY**
>
> Theologically speaking, when Christians speak of Mary they do so under one of two categories. A healthy Mariology tends to be either of these two:
>
> Christo-typical or Christ-centered Mariology, which seeks to explain Mary in light of her role in the life and mission of Jesus.
>
> Ecclesio-typical or Church-centered, which seeks to explain to the whole Church and its individual members what it means to be a faithful disciple of Jesus. Ideally whatever you can say about Mary, you should be able to say about the Church and yourself as a good Christian.

The most complete Christo-typical portrait of María in the whole of the Sacred Scriptures is found in the Gospel of Luke. He introduces her as the young virgin who accepts God's will in the event of the birth of Jesus and who prays with the Church at Pentecost. For Luke, she "is the ideal of the faithful Christian in her acceptance of the incarnation of Christ, believing the impossible to be true. She expressed true love

---

16. Cf. Jelly, "Mary and the Church," 435–58.

17. Kreitzer, *Reforming Mary*, 102.

18. Ibid., 103.

in visiting and serving Elizabeth."[19] She is the audacious woman of the Magnificat. She is a faithful member of the early Church, keeping vigil with the disciples in the upper room.

In two thousand years much has been written and said about this marvelous woman. Her importance has been exaggerated by some, while others have completely denied her. Some hold her as a valiant woman, while others see her as a subservient handmaid. She is the Madonna with Child of Christmas and the Sorrowful Mother of Good Friday, as well as the Faithful Disciple of Pentecost and the Radiant Woman of Revelation. Of the vast array of Mary images to pick from, for the purposes of this book, I will focus on María of the Magnificat[20] (see sidebar).

To understand the Magnificat, we need to remember María of Nazareth as living in a part of the world that had been conquered and dominated by Rome. Imperial soldiers were everywhere, and the poor were legion. María and her family lived in Nazareth, a town most Judeans had never even heard of. They were among the poor that longed for God to liberate them from their oppressors. As a woman from the scorned town of Nazareth, María's "story embodies God's preferential option for

---

MAGNIFICAT:
MARY'S HYMN OF PRAISE
(Luke 1:46–55)

My soul proclaims the greatness the Lord,
my spirit rejoices in God, my Savior.

For God looks on the lowliness of his servant,
henceforth all generations will call me blest.
The Almighty does great things for me,
and holy is his name.

From age to age, God has mercy on those who fear him.
God shows might with his arm, scattering the proud-hearted;

God casts the mighty from their thrones,
lifting up the lowly.
God fills the starving with good things,
sending the rich away empty.

God protects Israel, his servant, remembering his mercy,
the mercy promised to our ancestors,
for Abraham and his children for ever.

---

19. Ibid., 102.

20. The translation of the Magnificat found in the sidebar is based on *The New American Bible*, *The Greek Interlinear New Testament*, and an inclusive-language translation used by the Cistercians of Australia and New Zealand as found in Peters, *Liturgy*.

the poor and challenges economically advantaged people to be converted to their cause."[21]

We know well the story of the Annunciation and María's acceptance of God's proposal, despite its repercussions. When she finds herself a pregnant and unwed teenager, she leaves town. As much as we would like to think of María valiantly going to Judea to the aid of her cousin Elizabeth, she was probably sent somewhere to hide the family's shame (at least for a few months). As my colleague New Testament scholar Barbara Reid recounts, "In a tight-knit community of friends and kin, there would have been rumors, suspicion, false conclusions, gossip, and ostracism."[22] And yet María—poor, oppressed, pregnant, and alone— finds herself singing God's praises. With her Magnificat she "articulates an alternate ordering of life in God's realm by means of prophetic song (Luke 1:46–55). In this way "she prefigures the prophetic nature of Jesus' own ministry."[23] She also prefigures the Church's prophetic ministry on behalf of the poor and oppressed through works of charity or by denouncing social injustice.

The Christian faithful need to seriously consider the social implications of María's words. She is not merely singing a hymn of praise, she is offering a challenge. She is opening our eyes to God's liberating and powerful action. God brings down those who are in power and leaves the rich empty. God empowers the lowly and feeds the starving. But how does God do this? God does this through María's cooperation. God does it through the Church's cooperation. God does is through *us*, if we let him.

Cooperation with God's Reign is an essential ingredient to a liberating spirituality. No one can be liberated from sin without cooperating with God's action in his or her life. At the same time no one can help others be liberated from the consequences of sin without cooperating with God's Spirit. Luke presents the story of María in the light of the Spirit. In the first chapter of his Gospel the Spirit fills María,[24] Elizabeth, the child within her womb, and her husband, Zechariah. This is the same Spirit that according to Luke fills the Church on the day of Pentecost (Acts 2:4). Filled with the Spirit, María, Elizabeth, John, Zechariah, and the Church proclaim God's praises and bring people back to God and the

21. Johnson, *Truly Our Sister*. 37.

22. Reid, *Taking Up the Cross*, 105.

23. Ibid., 102.

24. Cf. Ibid., 103.

OVERSHADOWED BY GOD'S SPIRIT

According to Luke's Gospel, Mary is told by Gabriel that she would give birth to a son because of God's Spirit. While Elizabeth, Zechariah, and their son are filled with the Spirit, Mary is overshadowed by the Spirit. This is a notable difference because, as Barbara Reid points out, Luke compares the overshadowing (*episkiazein*) of Mary by God's spirit with God's presence coming down (*episkiazein*) upon the meeting tent where Israel kept the ark of the covenant (Exod 40:35). Mary becomes the ark of the new covenant in Christ.

ways of justice, meaning the liberation offered by God's Reign.

Overshadowed by the Spirit (see sidebar), María sings God's praise. She assumes her role as mother of Christ as "she assumes a broader role as a minister of salvation for the whole human race."[25] María's hymn of praise is also meant to be the song of the Church, of the people committed to the salvation of the whole world and the establishment of right relationships. These right relationships are established when the mighty are brought low and the lowly are raised up. This does not mean that they switch places. God's Reign is established when everyone is put on equal footing before God. In God's presence there are no rich or poor, mighty or lowly, rather, all are one as descendants of the promise given to Abraham and our ancestors.

Christians committed to liberation from sin and all its personal and social consequences have a special love for the Magnificat. In it they find Luke's Mariam to be a woman whose "role of denouncing oppression and critically proclaiming liberation in the name of God's mercy puts her in solidarity with their efforts."[26] Luke's Gospel claims that in the home of María and Joseph, Jesus grew in wisdom and age and favor before God and people (Luke 2:52–52). From them, he learned the importance of solidarity with the efforts of liberation in proclaiming God's Reign. Through him, they became the first among the Christian saints in the great communion of saints that he established in his blood spilled for the salvation (liberation from sin and healing of its consequences) of all people.

25. Bauer, *Essential Mary*, 6.
26. Johnson, *Truly Our Sister*, 56.

THE COMMUNION OF SAINTS

The Apostles' Creed includes the statement "I believe in the communion of saints." Historically, this statement was added as a description of the holy catholic Church. The holy catholic Church is a universal church extended over the earth. No matter what their social location or racial/ethnic origin, the baptized are united to one another in Christ. The *Catechism of the Catholic Church* explains that the communion of saints is meant to also be a communion of faith, communion of sacraments, communion of charisms, and a communion of charity (*CCC* 949–53). All of these communions are meant to be a communion of goods (*CCC* 947, 952) where all Christians are willing to place what they have and possess at the disposal and service of their brothers and sisters in the Lord in solidarity with all people, living and dead.

The Church excludes no one living or dead who believes in Christ and professes him as Lord and Savior. Those who believe and are baptized are saints, or rather they are sanctified. A faulty understanding of Christian spirituality claims that sanctification is a liberation from the cares of this world so that Christians can be like Christ concerned with the things of heaven. But if the Son of God did not care for this world, would he ever have been incarnated?

As Christians we believe that God's Son became one of us precisely because he was concerned with this world and with establishing God's Reign in this world. In Christ, heaven comes to earth and earth joins with heaven. And so, those who are joined to Christ in baptism belong to heaven and earth and should be concerned with both and build communion in both.

As Church doctrine developed, the communion of saints took on a more transcendental meaning than just the communion of all who believe in Christ across national, social, and ethnic lines. The communion of saints is concerned with the saints who find themselves all around the world today, but at the same time it is concerned with the saints who find themselves in purgatory and those who are already glorified in heaven. For if Jesus is Lord of the living and the dead, then the living and the dead are joined in eternal communion. How is this true? I do not want to venture a guess; suffice it to say that the communion of saints is a mystery. It joins together Christians who are in purgation, illumination, and union into the one household of God extended through time and space.

This eternal household is a household that cares for its members as well as for the world that Jesus came to save. And like every household, its members are at different places when it comes to maturity and commitment to the *familia*. The glorified saints are "the assembly of the firstborn enrolled in heaven" (Heb 12:23) and are probably the most mature and committed to the *familia*, and because of this they do not simply hang around the clouds strumming on harps and guitars all day. Rather, thanks to the singular mediation of Jesus Christ, they "intercede with the Father for us. . . . So by their fraternal concern is our weakness greatly helped" (*CCC* 956).

Many of the saints, like Rosa de Lima, Thérèse de Lisieux, and Toribio Romo (see sidebar), already "enrolled in heaven" also act as examples and role models for the saints still on earth. They are lifted up or rather canonized by the Church because the experience of their lives "shows that liberation from sin through cooperation (*synergia*) with the grace of Christ or the Holy Spirit leads to a renewal of spiritual life (Gal 2:2; Col 3:10) and growth in love of God and neighbor."[27]

Canonized saints like Francis and Clare of Assisi, Martín de Porres, and Theresa of Calcutta teach us that besides dedicating ourselves to God, as Christians we need to care for the people of this world, especially the poor and downtrodden. Many saints and Christian movements have committed themselves to concern for the

---

St. Toribio Romo

Besides praying for us and giving us the example of their lives, some of the saints in heaven continue to serve the needy on this earth. Such is the case of Toribio Romo, a Mexican priest who at the age of twenty-eight was martyred during the Cristero wars of the 1920s.

In the 1970s, a mysterious stranger began to come to undocumented immigrants lost in the desert. He would care for them and help them cross the border into the United States. He also gave them food, water, money, and suggestions for locating work. In return he would ask them to come visit him if they ever went back to Mexico. Many who returned discovered that the man who helped them was Toribio Romo González, Mexican martyr. He was canonized by Pope John Paul II in the year 2000. To this day, he continues his ministry to poor immigrants.

---

27. Ciobotea, "Salvation," 823.

world and its people by being liberated of all those things that keep them from serving Christ in the poor. They have learned that "Love of neighbor is the indispensable way to salvation."[28] In the work of liberation, Christians are liberated from their own sinful egoism so they can help heal and liberate others from the consequences of social, economic, and political sin.

ONE HOLY CATHOLIC AND APOSTOLIC CHURCH

In the Apostles' Creed, the communion of saints describes the Church. In the Nicene Creed the Church is described as being one, holy, catholic, and apostolic. These four adjectives tell us what we are supposed to be. At the same time they challenge us to be who we are called to be. They are our Christian vocation as individual believers and as Church.

> This is the sole Church of Christ, which in the Creed we profess to be one, holy, catholic, and apostolic. These four characteristics, inseparably linked with each other, indicate essential features of the Church and her share in God's mission. The Church does not possess them of herself; it is Christ who, through the Holy Spirit, makes his Church one, holy, catholic, and apostolic, and it is he who calls her to realize each of these qualities. (*CCC* 811)

Because it is a communion of saints it is one. It is the mystical body of Christ: "The mission of Christ and the Holy Spirit is brought to completion in the Church, which is the Body of Christ and the Temple of the Holy Spirit" (*CCC* 737). This Church is larger than one Christian denomination; it is all Christian denominations united in one faith, one hope, and one love. While the Catholic Catechism admits to wounds that have hurt this unity over the centuries, it also confirms that all the baptized in Christ are brothers and sisters in the one body of Christ. Living one baptism and sharing one Spirit, Protestants, Catholics, Orthodox, evangelical, and nondenominational Christians are called to evangelize the world and offer it the liberation that only Christ can give. We cannot do this if we are fighting among ourselves. The world will be a better place when Christians learn to work together as brothers and sisters in Christ.

Because it is a communion of saints it is holy. Like Israel, the Church is called to be holy because God is holy (Lev 19:2). The book of Leviticus explains what it means to be holy by inviting us to right relationships

28. Ibid., 823.

(justice) with God, our parents, and our neighbors. Holiness is especially concerned with not hoarding up goods for oneself at the expense of the poor. On the contrary, holy people provide for the poor (Lev 19:9–10).

Jesus gives this invitation to holiness a new twist when in Matthew's Gospel (5:48) he asks his followers to be perfect like God is perfect. This is a tall order, but it is not unattainable. In reading chapter 5 of Matthew's Gospel we find that true perfection comes from loving your enemies and those who do not necessarily love you. God is good to everyone whether they deserve it or not. Jesus further explains perfection as being attained by selling what you have, giving to the poor, and following him (Matt 19:21).

In Luke's Gospel (6:36) the injunction to holiness is to be merciful like God is merciful. Like perfection, this comes from loving your enemies and those who do not love you. It also comes from being helpful to those who cannot pay you back or do the same for you. Luke's Gospel describes Christian discipleship in terms of bringing good news to the poor and helping those in need. Therefore it should come as no surprise that to be like God we must learn how to help those who cannot repay us.

Because it is a communion of saints it is catholic. Often when we hear the word *catholic*, we think of the Roman Catholic Church, this however is not the intent of the Apostles' or Nicene Creeds, which are proclaimed by most Christian denominations. *Catholic* with a little *c* "means 'universal,' in the sense of 'according to the totality' or 'in keeping with the whole'" (CCC 830). Fundamentally this means the Church is universal in keeping with being the one body of Christ united to its head (Jesus). At the same time, while it is the whole body of Christ it is also sent to bring the Good News of Christ Jesus to the whole world. Its catholic identity therefore makes it missionary, inviting all men and women to communion with the Most Holy Trinity. Two thousand years of missionary activities teach us that the Gospel is best proclaimed by works of charity, liberation, and justice.

Because it is a communion of saints it is apostolic. The missionary activity lived by the Church makes it apostolic, in communion over the centuries with the original twelve apostles and seventy-two disciples of Christ. Countless numbers of men and women saints have joined these original saints. While it is true that the direct descendants of the apostles are those Christians called to serve as bishops, the Catholic Catechism reminds us that all Christians are called to the apostolate no matter what their Christian calling in the world. Being Christian is a vocation, it is a calling to an evangelical way of life, and this implies commitment to God's Reign and God's will "on earth as it is in heaven."

IN CONCLUSION

As Christians we are members of a large household that follows Jesus Christ, the great liberator (*CCC* 457, 530). Each one of us is called to grow in the Spirit of God so as to be faithful and life-giving members of his *familia*. We do not do this alone. To borrow from John Dunne, "no disciple of Jesus is an island entire of itself; every Christian is a member of the Church, a part of Christ's body."

As members of a body that is one, holy, catholic, and apostolic, we will necessarily come into contact with any number of individuals and groups of persons who will help us grow as Christians in the world. In this chapter we have considered the communion of persons we call God—Father, Son, and Holy Spirit—as well as the communion of saints: María, the saints, and the Church. We have seen that God has a preferential love for those the world despises and yet God does not hate the world. On the contrary, God so loves the world that he came to liberate it from sin and triumph over its consequences: material deprivation, unjust oppression, physical and psychological illness, and death. Taking our cue from God, the communion of saints "has not ceased to work for their [those who are oppressed by poverty] relief, defense, and liberation through numerous works of charity which remain indispensable always and everywhere" (*CCC* 2448).

So far in this book, we have considered liberating spirituality as a pilgrimage and journey of spiritual growth. We have looked at ourselves as body, soul, and spirit called to embrace the reality that surrounds us. We have also been invited to embrace the reality of God's liberating reign in our lives and in our world. For this reason we have considered what we believe about God and the communion saints in the spirit of liberation. As we continue with our book we will touch upon God's Word as the content that informs a Christian liberating spirituality in the next chapter and in our last chapter, we will consider the pillars that comprise it.

DISCUSSING CHAPTER 3

Questions about the Material

Who is God?

What is the Magnificat?

What is the communion of saints?

What are the four marks of the Church?

Questions about Your Own Experience

How is your relationship with God?

What is your experience of the communion of saints?

How is being Christian your calling (vocation) in the world?

How can belonging to the Church help you with your call to be Christian?

4

God's Formative Word

IN OUR PREVIOUS CHAPTER we considered those who participate in our spiritual growth. This chapter will consider the content that informs and assists our spiritual growth, God's formative Word. As we walk the journey of a liberating spirituality in the world, we find that we need to get in touch with the content of our Christian faith. This content is God's active Word, or God's self-revelation and how it impacts us. God's self-revelation and how it impacts us in our *cotidiano* (everydayness) is what this chapter is all about. The chapter will be divided into two sections. First we will look at where we as Christians find God's Word (Jesus), and then we will focus our attention on how we can use Sacred Scripture, especially the four Gospels, for our personal and communal formation.

FINDING GOD'S ACTIVE WORD

One of the most beautiful works of art in the Christian West is Michelangelo's ceiling in the Sistine Chapel. It is primarily comprised of nine scenes from the book of Genesis. These scenes, especially the creation of Adam, are so powerful that we can easily ignore the twelve colossal figures that are a part of the ceiling. These are the prophets and sibyls who, according to Michelangelo, foretold the coming of a universal savior. As Christians, we are familiar with the prophets, but do not know the sibyls. Quite simply, they are oracles or prophetesses of the ancient Greco-Roman world and representatives of Greek philosophy. But what do Greek philosophy and pagan oracles have to do with Christianity? Plenty, as far as the first chapter of John's Gospel is concerned.

When early Christians began to move out of Palestine, they found themselves immersed in a world that admired Greek thought and education. And even though the Mediterranean world was dominated by Rome, the academic language of the time was Greek. So it is that the

New Testament came to be written in Greek and not Latin or Hebrew. For us today, this means that in order to understand the New Testament, we need to familiarize ourselves with some Greek concepts and words. Such is the case for the word *logos*.

Logos is a philosophical and religious concept that is hard to express in our contemporary translations of the Gospel. Most English language Bibles simply translate it as Word, but it is not just any word, it is God's creative word. For the Greek philosophers, *logos*, like the Hebrew concept of wisdom (*sophia*),[1] was the creative principle that gave logic and harmony to all of existence. *Logos* is the act of talking things into being and order. Early Christians had no quarrel with this. Quite the contrary, they adopted it, making Jesus the fulfillment not only of the Jewish prophets and patriarchs but also of the Gentile sibyls and philosophers.

In the New Testament, St. Paul alludes to the *Logos* when he calls Jesus the "power of God and the wisdom of God" (1 Cor 1:24) and "the image of God" (2 Cor 4:4; Col 1:15). Rather than use the philosophical language of the *Logos*, Paul, being a good Jew, associates Christ with Wisdom, who is "the refulgence of eternal light, the spotless mirror of the power of God, the image of his goodness" (Wisdom 7:26).

John the Evangelist, on the other hand, adopts the term *Logos* without hesitation. Of the four Gospels, John's Gospel is the most symbolic and mystical. He is concerned with presenting Christ Jesus not just as the man from Nazareth, but as the preexistent and incarnate Word of God, which is to say, the *Logos*. He begins his Gospel with the news: "In the beginning was the Word [*Logos*], and the Word was with God, and the Word was God" (John 1:1). He goes on to boldly proclaim "the Word [*Logos*] became flesh and made his dwelling among us" (1:14). John's amazing news is the Good News the Greek philosophers of his day found hard to accept. Greek philosophy was dualistic and tended to divide reality into the soul, which was good, and matter, which was bad. The idea that the *Logos* would take on something material like flesh was inconceivable. Still, the Evangelist borrows the concept of *Logos* from the pagan philosophies in order to proclaim Jesus as God's Word active in the world.

For John and the early Church, Jesus the Christ is action. He is God's creative presence in the world. More than a noun or adjective, *Logos* is a verb, which is why in Latin Jesus is known as the *Verbum Dei*, which

1. Espín, "*Logos*/Word," 786.

translates as Word (*Verb*) of God. With the word *logos*, John attempts to reconcile Jewish and Greco-Roman religions and philosophies by claiming that Jesus of Nazareth, the *Logos* made flesh, is the fulfillment of both. He is the *Sophia* of God. This was good and scandalous news to both. On the one hand, Jewish religion could not fathom God becoming human, and Greco-Roman religion could not imagine the divine taking on something as base as human flesh. And yet, the *Logos* (*Verbum Dei*) who had created and ordered the universe had recently come into the world of humanity as one of us. In addition, he came not as a subject to be adored but as a verb to form, serve, and save us. He is the active Word of God that cannot be limited to a book, but is poured out into the person of Jesus and into the persons that form his body the Church. "And the *Logos* became flesh."

THE THREE BOOKS OF GOD'S WORD

God's Word cannot be limited to a single book, and those who want to limit it to the Sacred Scriptures turn the Bible into an idol by insisting that it alone contains God's revelation to us. Idols cannot see, hear, or speak; they cannot save. God's Word, on the other hand, saves because it is a verb, a creative, saving, liberating, and sanctifying Word that cannot be contained in a single book. Thanks to the illuminative effort of the Triple Way mentioned in chapter 1, God's Word enlightens us and breaks into our world in the *cotidiano* we call life. For this reason, God's Word will not be limited to a single book. On the contrary, like God, who is triune (three in one), God's Word is also triune. The Catholic Catechism reminds us that in meditating upon God's Word we usually turn to books such as "the Sacred Scriptures, particularly the Gospels, holy icons, liturgical texts of the day or season, writings of the spiritual fathers, works of spirituality, the great book of creation, and that of history, the page on which the 'today' of God is written" (*CCC* 2705). Borrowing from the work of St. Bonaventure, we discover God's active Word or better God's Verb is found primarily in three books: the Book of Creation, the Book of Scriptures, and the Book of History. These three books make up the Word of God and contain a variety of material. They also correspond to the context, content, and processes of the spiritual life and are ways in which we are able to see, judge, and act in the world. Let's look at these books in no particular order; they are each important in their own right.

The Book of Scriptures

Book of Creation	Book of Scriptures	Book of History
	Sacred Scripture (Bible)	
	Catechism and theology	
	Spiritual writing	
	Fine arts (music, painting, etc)	
	Novels and poetry	
	News media	
	Judge	
	Content	

When I mention the Book of Scriptures to people, they tend to immediately think of the Bible or, better, the Sacred Scriptures, and certainly these are the Scriptures par excellence, and they are what we use to judge or measure all other forms of scripture. Still, as mentioned in article 2705 of the Catholic Catechism they are not the only scriptures that God uses to reveal himself or his message to us. Our Church has produced countless works by theologians, mystics, and spiritual writers. God's Word is found in our creeds, catechisms, canon law, treatises, tracts, hymns, and poetry. It is an overflowing and abundant Word that has inspired writers like Dionysius, Benedict, Augustine, Hildegard, Clare and Francis of Assisi, Martin Luther, Teresa de Avila, Leo XIII, Dorothy Day, and César Chávez, to name a few.

We cannot, however limit the scriptures to the Bible, theology, prophetic, or spiritual writing. The Book of Scriptures is writ large, and as such it is all types of human expression such as writing, music, painting, and other arts and crafts. How often, while reading a good book, listening to a great song, or admiring a beautiful work of art, have you felt something stir within you? Your heart burns as God's Word makes itself known. The trick is to allow yourself to be stirred; to hear the fire that is being kindled in your heart. You need to form a Spirit-thirsty heart so that as you read the scripture—be it the Bible, a novel, a comic book, or the local news—God's Word will touch and move you. A Spirit-thirsty heart is one that seeks the Spirit of God in all things and at the same time is led by God's Spirit. This is a heart that does not relegate God to Sundays and the Bible, but rather is open to encountering God in the *cotidiano* (day to day existence) and in all human expression. A Spirit-thirsty heart is a heart that contemplates and appreciates the awesomeness of God's creative and active Word.

A Spirit-thirsty heart along with a knowledge-hungry mind will stand in awe before a painting or sculpture (it need not be religious art) and feel the humanity that went into it, hear the God that whispered into the artist's ears, and be stirred by the Spirit that stirred the artist. Let yourself be moved. Literature and the arts, whether masterful or commonplace, are vehicles of human expression and instruments of God's Word. They are not just the fruit of creative humans but mirrors of the Creator of us all. All of these concrete expressions of the human spirit can be places where God speaks to us if only we learn to follow our Spirit-thirsty hearts.

The Book of Creation

Book of Creation	Book of Scriptures	Book of History
Nature	Sacred Scripture (Bible)	
Human nature	Catechism and theology	
Society	Spiritual writing	
Culture	Fine arts (music, painting, etc)	
Religion	Novels and poetry	
Community	News media	
See	Judge	
Context	Content	

While we need to learn to stand in awe before human expressions, creation often simply grabs our attention and takes our breath away. The Book of Creation is constantly open before us, and in it we discover God's loving presence and creativity. In it St. Bonaventure and other spiritual writers and theologians invite us to see God's mission as *bonum diffusivum* (self-diffusing goodness). Creation is God's way of sharing the wealth, so to speak. It flows from the fountain of God's generosity and providence, and it is the context in which we live our lives. It is the fruit of God's love, and in it we humans discover the fruit that nourishes our bodies, souls, and spirits. Through nature God gives us what our nature needs.

The Book of Creation is a twofold reality: the nature of creation and our own human nature. It is all that is natural and bountiful springing forth into a culture of life. Life, however, is a process of growth and development that slowly evolves over time. It moves towards completion in God. As the Franciscan theologian Zachary Hayes reminds us, "Created existence, therefore, is a dynamic reality, directed in its inner core to a fulfillment and completion which is to be the mysterious fruit of its history."[2]

Like the Book of the Scriptures, the Book of Creation has a number of manifestations. These come from God's creative hand or from human creativity, and they are nature, society, culture, religion, and community.

- *Nature* is the physical/material order in which we exist. In the case of human nature it is also the deep-seated character or essence that can motivate behavior.

- *Society* is an economic, social, and industrial structure that help people create a place in which to live together in relative peace and well-being in a particular territory.

- *Culture* comes from the Latin *colere*, which means to cultivate. It is a series of patterned behaviors, symbolic expressions, and symbols that give life meaning for a particular group of people.

- *Religion* comes from the Latin *religere*, that is, "to bind together." It is a set of tenets, beliefs, and rituals that help unite people to each other and to the Sacred Other, which many religions call God.

- *Community* denotes a group of people living in close proximity and sharing common ideals and goals. Communities can take the forms of families, religious communities, cities, and so forth.

With the exception of nature, these are human and plural creations. There is no one human society, culture, religion, or community, but a variety of societies, cultures, religions, and communities. Though created by human beings, they manifest God's love of diversity of expression and reveal God's manifold wisdom. How liberating it would be to understand that in God diversity is not division, but rather a bountiful harvest found in the Book of Creation.

"Creation is the mirror in which we can see, feel, hear, taste, and smell God and not just things around us. Bonaventure, in fact, encourages all sciences to uses the physical senses as well [as] reason to study the reality in which we live, not to gather up a bunch of facts but to get

---

2. Z. Hayes, *Hidden Center,* 13.

at truth."[3] This truth is found in God's plan of salvation as it reveals itself through history.

The Book of History

Book of Creation	Book of Scriptures	Book of History
Nature	Sacred Scripture (Bible)	His/Her-story
Human Nature	Catechism and theology	My/Your-story
Society	Spiritual writing	Our-story
Culture	Fine arts (music, painting, etc)	Church History
Religion	Novels and poetry	Secular History
Community	News media	Life
See	Judge	Act
Context	Content	Process

The Book of Scriptures is the content that helps us judge the Book of Creation or the context in which we live our lives. The Book of History, on the other hand, is the story of the various processes used by people to put the Word of God into action over time. The Book of Creation has a long history, and in this history is found any number of histories. Like the other two books of God's Word, the Book of History has several manifestations or chapters, if you will. There are chapters on the Tradition of the Church, as well as the traditions of various peoples, cultures, and religions. Other chapters include the histories of our nations, religions, churches, families, and other communities.

Moreover, there are the chapters of all our personal histories or life stories and experiences. I like to think of the Book of History as being the book of his-story, her-story, your-story, my-story, and so on and so forth. In other words, it is the book of life and all its stories and experiences. All of these chapters in the Book of History are revelatory of who God is and who God wants us to be.

History or life is often described as a journey. For us Christians, this journey is a pilgrimage undertaken as disciples of Jesus. The disciples have been many and varied over the centuries, and like the early disciples journeying on the road home to Emmaus (Luke 24:13–35), they have often found themselves with the stranger who is God, Emmanuel, Jesus. A cherished line from Luke's story is, "Were not our hearts burning

---

3. Cavazos-González, "Spirituality of Study," 73.

(within us)?" (Luke 24:32). The disciples in the story of Emmaus ask this of each other when they discover the truth of the stranger as the risen Lord. In this way they acknowledged that their journey was a revelatory one. In "their-story" they discovered the truth of God's living Word. We need to be able to do the same in our stories, our lives and experience. It is here and now that we come face to face with the incarnate Word of God.

GOD'S WORD IS INCARNATIONAL

For us Christians the three books of God's Word (*Verb*) show a creative, active, and loving God who desires us intensely. God not only wants us to serve and follow him, God wants us to love him and let ourselves be loved by him. So intense is God's love and desire for us that it takes on human flesh in the person of Jesus of Nazareth. As previously noted, Jesus Christ is the incarnate *Logos*, the Word made flesh. This is an important and central teaching in Christianity and can never be forgotten or ignored. However, more than just a doctrine to believed, it somehow must be lived.

After chapter 1, the remainder of John's Gospel and the rest of the New Testament never again mention the *Logos*. Instead, the Christian Scriptures focus their attention on the life of Jesus and the early Church. The philosophical concept of *Logos* and the Hebrew idea of *Sophia* blend into one in the person of Jesus of Nazareth, who is the incarnate and living Word of God. And, with the breath of Jesus (the Holy Spirit) deep in the lungs of the faithful, they too incarnate the liberating power of God's Word in their lives and deeds.

Christians find God's Word in the Sacred Scripture and yet do not limit God's revelation to that particular book. On the contrary, Christians read God's Word everywhere, because it is a living Word; the creative *Logos* and illuminating *Sophia* found in the Book of Creation and the Book of History as well as the Book of Scriptures. And what we read we are called to ponder and meditate upon. Our reflection must spur us to incarnate God's Word in our own lives, contexts, and circumstances. The Gospel must sink into our gut, and for this reason Christians are called to read God's Word wherever they find it with a knowledge-hungry mind and a Spirit-thirsty heart. In regard to God's Word, Christians today need to recover a sense of study as an ongoing spiritual exercise that keeps the mind and heart connected.[4] In this way the mind and heart are free to serve God and neighbor.

The Christian mind and heart must work with each other if ever our beliefs are going to Christianize our actions and gut reactions. For this reason, Christian tradition gives us two ways of studying God's Word: lectio divina and revision of life. We will now focus our attention on how we can use Sacred Scripture, especially the four Gospels to be formed in a liberating spirituality.

COMMUNAL LECTIO DIVINA

I have had the pleasure of working with various Scripture study groups in the United States, Mexico, and Italy. The most fruitful method of Scripture study that I have found is one I learned from theologian, storyteller, and spiritual writer Megan McKenna. Megan has graduate degrees in both Scripture and systematic theology, but much of her wisdom comes from the work she has done with the Christian community around the world. In her travels and ministry, she spent some time with the Comunidades de Base in Central America. It was there that she came in contact with the method of Scripture study that I learned from her. Over a span of twenty-something years, I have had the opportunity to use it and reshape it based on what I have learned from various evangelization, charismatic, and other types of small home-based communities. I have chosen to call this method a communal lectio divina, and it is based on the theological reflection that the Church over the centuries has referred to as lectio divina or spiritual reading.

Lectio divina (literally divine reading) implies "listening to the Sacred Scriptures."[5] It is a method of seeking to be illuminated or enlightened through a meditative reading and conversation with God, which can be traced back to the early patristic period (100–500 AD). No one really knows who originated it or when it began to be practiced as a group exercise in theological reflection. Some historians claim that lectio divina as a communal exercise first began with the Spanish Bishop Isidro de Sevilla (560–636).[6] This may or may not be true, but we do know that this saintly bishop recommended that reading the Sacred Scripture be

---

4. Cf. Ibid., 71.

5. Pennington, "Wisdom," 1043.

6. Holmes, *History of Christian Spirituality*, 50.

done in community, saying that it is more fruitful to read the Scriptures in a group.

Over the centuries, lectio divina, which is a conversation with God, became a private and individual monastic dialogue, which can take place either in the solitude of one's cell or silently within a group setting in a chapel. The Latin American version has the community and not just the individual enter into dialogue with God and each other. This emphasizes the *cotidianidad* of God's Word in people's lives. Often it is done in people's living rooms rather than in chapels or classrooms. In either case it still follows the stages of traditional lectio divina.

Lectio divina, or reading God, is meant to be "an agreeable and delectable reading. It is tasting the Verb, tasting God in the Holy Spirit who enlivens the reading and who elicits in the reader a secret gusto so that s/he may situate him/herself in harmony with what s/he has read and respond with prayer and her/his whole life to the Word of God."[7] Traditionally, lectio divina is done in three stages known as *lectio, meditatio*, and *oratio* (reading, meditating, and praying), and it is meant to be a relational and fruitful encounter with God rather than theological study or a critical biblical interpretation. Let's look briefly at each of these stages before considering the questions used for communal lectio divina.

Lectio (Reading)

The communal lectio divina begins with the proclamation of a Scripture passage, normally the Gospel for the coming Sunday. The proclamation leads to a sharing of answers to various discussion questions (found below). Everyone is invited to answer based on his or her experience and knowledge. Exegesis, historical criticism, and other biblical tools are not necessary unless, of course, they are part of your lived experience. Imagination, one's life story, and communal sharing are essential to this type of Lectio. In this way the written Word of God found in the Bible encounters the lived Word of God found in the community's experience and the experiences of its members.

- Imagination helps one enter into the story or passage being read. It helps one imagine how the characters in the text must have felt.

---

7. Colombas, *Diálogo com Deus*, 47. The translation is my own.

- One's life story is filled with events and happenings that may be similar to what is written in the text. These life events can help make the characters in the text more real.

- Communal sharing on the text can help break it open in ways that one person would never have thought possible.

Since the Word of God is a living word, it is best to have it proclaimed out loud. One or several readers proclaim the passage as often as needed during the lectio divina (usually between questions). Unless you are hard of hearing, the first proclamation is best listened to with personal copies of *the Scriptures closed and hearts open*. Individuals are free to open their Scriptures after the first question has been answered. I have found that it is best not to all use the same translation. Instead, it adds to the discussion of the Scripture if participants have differing translations and languages of the Scripture.

Meditatio (Meditating)

Participants mull over God's Word out loud by answering the questions (found below). As previously mentioned, the answers to the questions need to come from what each has heard, experienced, and learned in life. Human beings have not changed much over the centuries, and often one's feelings and doubts are the same feelings and doubts experienced by the people in the Gospel stories.

Take, for example, the Virgin María. According to the Gospel of Luke, María pondered over the mysteries she saw unraveling before her in her son's life. Many a mother can probably share the feelings and emotions María felt as she carried, birthed, and nurtured the child Jesus. Sadly, many mothers also know what it is like to see their children misjudged, ridiculed, and even murdered. These women are able to reflect, meditate, and even contemplate the Gospel story through María's eyes. The Church highly recommends that our *meditatio* use these three ways of thinking: reflection, meditation, and contemplation.

In brief, reflection is thinking based on your experience and *cotidianidad*. It is looking at yourself in the mirror of how you feel and how you act and react. Meditation, on the other hand, is thinking about something you've heard or read. It is entering into something outside yourself with both the use of reason and the imagination. In the communal lectio divina you are invited to move beyond reflecting on how the Scripture touches you personally to enter into the Scripture itself and discover what it means in and of itself. In this way the Scripture can move you to action and ongoing conversion. Finally, contemplation is moving from thought to vision. It is looking for God in both the written Word and the experienced Word. Often contemplation is simply an "aha!" moment, a catching a glimpse of God in one's discussion or *cotidiano* in a brief moment of illumination and union with God.

Oratio (Praying)

When doing this type of *lectio*, we need to remember that believers do not read the Scriptures for information but for transformation and ongoing formation. This requires prayer. Each session begins and ends with prayer. It is important to begin by *invoking the Holy Spirit*. The same Spirit who inspired Matthew, Mark, Luke, and John and all the other writers of the Sacred Scriptures needs to be allowed to inspire each and every member of the community gathered to read and share that Scripture.

Usually the *lectio* ends with final spontaneous prayers of praise and/or intercession reflecting the meditation done on God's Word and the needs of the community. At first this type of prayer may seem hard to do, especially when not everyone in the sharing group knows each other. But as time goes on, the group that gathers weekly to break open God's Word with each other will become a community. When that happens, love and concern for each other will lead to an enriched closing prayer.

QUESTIONS FOR COMMUNAL LECTIO DIVINA

The home-based communities I have worked with normally share Scripture by reading the Gospel of the coming Sunday. Occasionally, another reading will be chosen in keeping with the circumstances the community is involved with at the time. I would like to explain each one using the reading of the Transfiguration (Luke 9:28–36). Let's turn now to consider the questions:

1. How does this passage make you feel?

2. Who, where, when, why, how? (and the negative of these).

3. Whom do you identify with in the passage? How do you think s/he was feeling when the events of the passage occurred?

4. Is there anything about this passage that puzzles or disturbs you? Does any of it cause you to question the passage or the reality in which you find yourself?

5. The Gospel deals with peace, health, justice, liberation and solidarity with the poor/marginalized (Luke 4:16–19). What is Jesus telling you that needs to concretely change or be bolstered in your life in light of this passage?

6. What is Jesus calling our community to do to respond positively and concretely to the Gospel in the light of peace, health, justice, liberation, and/or solidarity with the poor/marginalized?

7. What about this passage is good news for you?

1. How does this passage make you feel?

This and the last question need to be answered by everyone in the group. For this first question, close your books and listen to someone read the story of the Transfiguration. At the end of the *lectio* share with others how the passage makes you feel (in one or two words). There is no need to explain why.

Remember that thinking is not allowed. Feel the reading! In this day and age many people are out of touch with their feelings, which is why it is important that the leader challenge people to use only feeling words. I have come to find that even though there are many words to describe feelings and emotions, they all come down to being touched by four primary feelings or some variance of these: joy, sorrow, anger, or fear. Even love is touched by these. Love can make some people feel joyful, while it frightens others. Often it brings mixed feelings. In either case it is important that I get in touch with how I am feeling and how God's Word makes me feel.

In the case of the Transfiguration I may feel happy (joy). Perhaps I feel confused, which is a type of fear. Or maybe I feel left out, which is sorrow. Or possibly I don't like that Jesus took only Peter, James, and John and so I feel upset (angry).

2. Who, where, when, why, how? (and the negative of these)

This question invites the participants to *meditatio* or rather to break open the text or story by looking at what is going on, what is being said, who is saying it, and why. What do we know about the people involved? It also considers who is and isn't present in the Bible story or message being proclaimed. If there are more studious people in the group who can speak to some of the historical context of the story, let them; but do not let them dominate the discussion. Remember lived experience is more important than biblical theology for this type of lectio divina.

In the case of the Transfiguration story, I have heard communities discuss the presence of Jesus, Peter, James, and John. They have even talked about who Moses and Elijah were and what they meant to the Jews. The importance of law and prophecy can also become an interesting thing to talk about in reading this passage. Another interesting discussion is around who is not present at the scene. Why were the women and the other apostles not invited?

3. Whom do you identify with in the passage? How do you think s/he was feeling when the events of the passage occurred?

This and the fourth question flow quite naturally from the second question. Here is where your experience and imagination really come into the *meditatio*. In the story of the Transfiguration, for example, I like to identify with Peter's brother Andrew. From that perspective it strikes me that Jesus seems to have his favorites. Is that OK? Am I OK with that? And what is it about Peter, James, and John that would get them picked and not me, I mean Andrew. After all, in the Gospels of Matthew, Mark, and Luke, the disciples James, John, and Peter came to Jesus at the same time as Andrew. In John's Gospel (1:40), Peter met Jesus thanks to Andrew.

4. Is there anything about this passage that puzzles or disturbs you? Does any of it cause you to question the passage or the reality in which you find yourself?

There is an old saying that claims, "Jesus came to comfort the afflicted and afflict the comfortable." Over the years Christians have become very comfortable with the Gospel message. It is good news, after all. However, good news isn't always comfortable. At times it can prod and push us into directions and tasks that we may not naturally undertake. This is where this question comes into play. What about the Transfiguration, for example, bothers me? Perhaps it is that Jesus wanted his secret kept under wraps. Or maybe that Jesus seems to have favorites. Or perhaps that it reminds me that I sometimes play favorites or am not the favorite of someone special in my life.

Besides prodding me, the Gospel is often simply not something that I understand. I am not always familiar with the period or location or customs written about in the Scriptures. Maybe my experience or the experience of my community alone is not enough to grasp the full meaning and impact of the Bible. Maybe I need to do some further study, read a few books, or take a class.

5. The Gospel deals with liberation through peace, health, justice, and solidarity with the poor/marginalized (Luke 4:16–19). What is Jesus telling you that needs to concretely change or be bolstered in your life in light of this passage?

Questions 5 and 6 are the action/response (*actio*) questions in the lectio divina. These questions are often skipped when the members of the group are still getting to know each other. Question 5 is a very personal question, and question 6 presupposes that the group has actually become a community. Still, while they may be uncomfortable questions, they are important ones and in reality they are why Christians do lectio divina in the first place.

It may be that at the beginning of a group's journey together question 5 becomes a question for private meditation. It becomes homework so to speak, to go home and determine a concrete measurable response to the passage. It has to be more than simply saying I want to be better. It requires the question how? Based on what we have read and discussed, how does my life need to change? What one thing can I do during the week to put into practice this particular Gospel passage so that it becomes liberating? So I propose to work on one area of Jesus's mission as announced in Luke 4:16–19.

Going back to the example of the Transfiguration, perhaps what I need to do is not let it bother me when others get picked for something instead of me. And so, I propose to work on justice in the sense of right relationships and work on not getting angry when I feel rejected. Or maybe I choose to work on peace by spending more time with Christ on the mountain and so I propose to spend an hour with the Blessed Sacrament every week.

6. What is Jesus calling our community to do to respond positively and concretely to the Gospel of liberation in the light of peace, health, justice, and/or solidarity with the poor/marginalized?

As the group becomes a community, participants will need to occasionally share with each other the answer to question 5, and it will become natural for each of you to check with each other on how you did with what you proposed to do. So in the case of the Transfiguration story, the members of the community might ask me, "So how did you do? Did you feel rejected in the past week? Did you let it bother you or did you let it go?" Or they might want to know, "Did you spend an hour before the Blessed Sacrament?"

As this begins to happen, the community begins to really get to know each other and the contexts in which they find themselves. At this point the community needs to begin to focus on how they can respond to the Gospel together. I have seen communities set up soup kitchens as a response to the Gospel's call to solidarity with the poor. One community I know learned about natural remedies and herbs and set up a natural medicine pharmacy in the parish center to help people come to better health. Another community, made up entirely of retirees, decided they were called to keep up the parish's garden. In this way they brought peace through beauty. Another became active in an agency that advocated for social reforms in the city and worked for justice.

These are very different responses and are based on where the community finds itself and what the needs of its context are. It also is based on how much time, talent, and treasure a community is willing to commit to responding to God's Word together.

7. What about this passage is good news for you?

Even if other questions are skipped for the sake of time, this question is never skipped. Doing communal lectio divina, especially on the Gospel, should always be good news. Reviewing everything that you heard discussed and shared in this session, what comforts you? What makes you feel good or at peace? What did you like about the experience?

It is important to the development of community that this and the first question be answered by everyone in the group. Often groups simply go around the circle, to make sure everyone responds. People are always free to say "pass" if they are not ready to answer when it is their turn. In this case they are invited to respond when everyone else is done.

I have been doing this type of Lectio with various groups for over twenty years, first with my parishioners and an ecumenical pastor's group in San Antonio, Texas, and eventually with a prayer group in Rome. Now I meet occasionally with a small group of theology students. In each group this type of lectio divina has been a way to do theological and spiritual reflection. It is a simple method and can be done without the need of a priest, theologian, or Bible expert. Yet while it may be simple, it can be powerful and life changing. These questions are meant to help a group or community see, judge, and act (*ver, juzgar, y actuar*) in the various contexts in which they find themselves. It places our current experiences alongside the tradition of the Scriptures and brings them into conversation. It respects both life experience and the Scriptures as holders of God's Word. The Book of Scriptures and the Book of History meet so that together they can move those doing the lectio divina to improve the Book of Creation. In all of this we need to remember that as Christians we belief in the incarnate Word (*Verbo encarnado*) who is Jesus. Therefore, lectio divina is about getting to know Jesus as our way, truth, and life.

REENVISIONING LIFE

In the Gospel, we discover that Pontius Pilate sought to know Jesus during the Good Friday trial. However, Pilate's desire was motivated out of curiosity about this peculiar man and the need for power over him. Pilate asked, "What is truth?" yet his eyes were closed to Jesus—the way, the *truth*, and the life—because he did not love him. Pilate's encounter with the Lord was not life changing (as far as we know).

Christians, on the other hand, seek to know Jesus out of love, not curiosity or the desire for power. Our encounter with him is essentially life changing, which is why Christian Tradition calls us to ponder God's Word (*Verb*) with revision of life in mind. Over the centuries, this revision of life has been known as *metanoia*, conversion, penance, examination of conscience, and spiritual direction (to name a few).

The revision of life or examination of conscience is a blend of the purgative and illuminative efforts of the Triple Way. This is done through self-reflection and meditation on the Sacred Scripture, especially the Gospels. The unitive effort of the Triple Way is found in the ultimate purpose of the revision of life, which is to come to know God's Word and at the same time to allow God's Word to come to know me in intimate union with God. In this way I can produce fruit and incarnate God's creative and active Word (*Logos*) in my life.

Alexander Gaitan, a Claretian friend of mine from Colombia, shared with me a process for the revision of life. He first learned the method for the revision of life while in religious formation in Colombia. He shared it with me, and I have found it quite helpful in my life. I would like to share it with you. Ultimately this revision of life is a blend of the examination of conscience and spiritual direction. Recently as I discussed it with a group of students, I tweaked it and described it as a way to revise (modify or correct) and reenvision life. We decided to call the method "reenvisioning life." I would recommend that if you have a confessor or spiritual director that you use this five-step reenvisioning life process to prepare for your visits. It can certainly be used for private reflection; however, it is most fruitful when you have the opportunity to share it with one or two spiritual friends in a day of recollection or retreat or with your spiritual director.

This is a five-step method, and it presupposes that you have a Christian life project or rather a Christian calling in the world. Essentially, the life project or Christian calling is the primary way in which you publicly live your share in God's mission. Remember that all Christians, not just priests, nuns, or brothers, are called to witness to the Gospel with their lives. For this reason a Christian life project can be married life, priesthood, consecrated life, parenthood, lay ministry, social work, or some other form of Gospel witness.

The Reenvisioning Life Process

1. Getting in touch with how I am feeling.
2. Significant events in my recent life.
3. Gratitude for God's generous presence.
4. Jesus and the Scripture in my Life.
5. Discerning an Evangelical Response.

As I did with the communal lectio divina, allow me to elaborate a bit on the questions for the reenvisioning life process (see table). For the review of life you will need to reflect on a given period of time. You can review your day, week, month, year, or life, depending on when your last review of life was and why you are doing this review of life. For the sake of this explanation, let's say I am a married lay minister, and in the last month I got a new job that will require me to relocate. In talking with my spiritual friend I will focus on the period of the last month.

Getting in Touch with How I Am Feeling

There are a number of emotions and feelings that we experience in a month or any given period of time. Often this step is referred to as a check-in between two or three friends, and it is meant to help you "step back and gain perspective on life."[8] Looking over this past month, *what is my general feeling?* Have I been basically happy, sad, fearful, or angry? As mentioned above, most emotions are a variance of one of these or are touched by one or more of these four primary feelings. In either case, it is important that I get in touch with how I am feeling because it might explain how I have been acting or reacting this last month. For the sake of our argument, let's say that I have been generally happy and content with how things are going. I love my wife and *familia*, I enjoy helping out at the church, and my new job is great. However, the transfer makes me nervous and I have been a bit on edge.

Significant Events in My Recent Life

So many things can happen in a month or any given period of time. Most of them are probably not that significant; however, there are always one or two things that might strike you as worth looking at for better or worse. These are *kairos* moments, which is to say, God-filled moments,

8. Haase, *Living the Lord's Prayer,* 131.

and they need to be considered in light of your Christian life project. How do they enhance or detract from your calling in life? For example, in this last month my wife and I celebrated our wedding anniversary and I got a new job. The anniversary helped me reflect on my call as a married person to manifest God's love for the Church. Have I been doing this? Christ loved the Church enough to die for her; what sacrifices have I made for my wife and family? Is my job something that a Christian should be doing? How does the transfer enhance or detract from my commitment to God's people at my parish, at home? How can I witness to Christ at work? It might be too early to tell, so I can decide to keep a close watch on how this event of the last month will continue to play itself out. The important thing to remember is that I have a Christian life project, call, or vocation that needs nurturing and care.

Gratitude for God's Generous Presence

God is always active in our lives. Periodically we need to stop and reflect on where we have seen God's divine providence and generous hand. What am I grateful for? My family, my parish community, the pastor? Maybe I am especially grateful for my new job. How do I show my gratitude? Perhaps I had a Mass celebrated in thanksgiving for my marriage and new job. Or maybe I took my family out for a celebratory dinner. I might have even made a donation to a charitable cause in order share my good fortune with the less fortunate. The answers to these questions will tell me more about me than about God. "What are my values?" is really the underlying question here. We are usually most grateful for what we value and hold dear.

Back to the example of the new job. How you responded to getting the new job will help you determine if you see God at work in getting this new job, or in your marriage. This step in the method of reenvisioning life really touches the heart of your *cotidiano*. Do you relegate God to Church, Sunday, and the Bible? Or is God real in your everyday life? Is God in the humdrum routine, the special occasions, and the everyday reality of life? If so, are you grateful? How do you show it?

Jesus and the Scripture in my Life

Jesus Christ is the incarnate Verb, the creative and active Word of God made flesh, and so he speaks to us continually. Sadly, we simply do not always stop to listen. Reviewing my answers to the above three steps, what do I think Jesus is trying to tell me? What is he trying to make me realize? Why is he trying to get my attention? What does he want for my *familia*? Why did I get this job? Is there a Gospel or Bible story, quote, symbol that ties into how my life has been of late?

As regards to my marriage, I might envision Jesus making wine out of water at the wedding feast in Cana. I can feel that Jesus is just as present in my marriage as he was for the couple in Cana. If my new job is not really the work I want to do, I might think of the prodigal son feeding the swine. Or maybe this is my dream job, the one I have always desired, but I am afraid to mess it up. Perhaps the words "Fear not; I am with you" bring me comfort and ease my nervousness about moving to a new place. Maybe it's a really important job that I never even considered before, and so the stories of the Virgin María and other figures being invited to do the extraordinary are what come to mind.

In any case, do not over think this. Do not run to the Scriptures to look for something. Rather, allow the words, image, symbol, and/or story to come up from within your heart or spring up out of your gut. If you've been to church on a regular basis, you've heard and read the Sacred Scripture often enough that it resides deep in your unconscious, and it will surface when you need or look for it. Believe that Jesus will inspire you with a message. It may not be during your actual period for the reenvisioning life process. Oftentimes it is sometime later; when you least expect it, your heart or your gut gives you Jesus's message.

If you do receive a particular Scripture passage, story, or verse during the time you are with your spiritual friend, you might want to use some of the methodology of the communal lectio divina to help you explore God's message for you. In this way you can move towards action, or better, an evangelical response.

Discerning an Evangelical Response

The last step is that of discernment, and it builds off the first four steps. God's Word, whether it is God's Word as found in your life, in creation, or in the Scripture, demands a response that is evangelical. Lately, *evangelical* has become a loaded word. Often we associate it with fundamentalist Protestant Christianity, but the truth is all Christian churches are evangelical. *Evangelical* comes from the Greek word *evangelion* (*evangelio* in Spanish; *gospel* in English) meaning "good news." The reenvisioning life process has to be evangelical. It has to help me celebrate the good news in my life as well as move me to become good news for others. In this way I am liberated to help liberate others.

This does not happen in one sitting; reenvisioning life takes time and is a lifelong commitment. As I mentioned for the previous question, the answers often come after the actual reenvisioning life process is over. Such is the case for question 5. If you haven't finished with question 4 it might be hard to be concrete about question 5. Still it is important to walk away from your reenvisioning life process with some kind of proposed action. The details might not all be worked out, but an orientation can be established. Your answers to these questions require that your Christian life project be strengthened with some plan of action. Decide what to do and let God handle the details.

In the case of the new job as a married lay minister, you need to consider how your new job will touch the lives of others. How will you handle it? How will they handle it? You may have to transfer to another place. Can you take your loved ones with you? How will you stay in touch? Maybe you need to reconsider the new job? Or hopefully, the new job will not cause any problems for your living situation, but what will it do to your Church commitment? How will you better live the Gospel because of it? In either case, make sure that what you intend to do is what God is calling you to do. For this reason, this question requires discernment. In the meantime, I can discern that God is calling me to respond evangelically, by committing to a discernment process. Or I might feel moved to quit my job and find another one that is more suitable to the needs of my *familia* and parish community. Perhaps I might feel called to accept the transfer and make myself available to a new parish community in another city.

IN CONCLUSION

What the Hebrew prophets and the Greco-Roman sibyls sought to see and hear, we see and hear; the incarnate Word of God. We may not see and hear him as did the disciples and apostles in the Gospel stories, but with the eyes and ears of faith, we see and hear him.

In this chapter we have considered three books of God's Word: Scripture, Creation, and History. We have also looked at two ways in which we can use God's Word to help us become better Christians. We realize that not only are we called to read all about the incarnate Verb, we are asked to see, hear, and touch that Word.

God's creative and active Word sees, hears, and touches us. It demands action that is evangelical—good news to the poor, the infirm, the oppressed and marginalized (Luke 4:16–19). Reading, reflecting, meditating, and contemplating God Word is meant to be a formative and transformative experience. In the next chapter we will consider how that formation is lived out through the pillars of a liberating spirituality.

DISCUSSING CHAPTER 4

Questions about the Material

What are the three books of the Word of God?

What is the *Logos, Sophia*?

What are the four primary feelings?

Questions about Your Own Experience

What is your relationship with the Word of God?

What is your experience of lectio divina? Bible study?

How can the reenvisioning life process help your spiritual life?

How can reflection on God's Word improve your Christian vocation?

5

Pillars of Liberating Spirituality*

A S WE SAW IN the previous chapter, God's Word demands work. It requires us to use evangelical and liberating action to transform and renew not just individuals but the whole world. For that reason, Christian theology has been about liberation since the day Jesus unraveled the scroll of Isaiah in his hometown's synagogue (Luke 4:16–21). On that day Jesus opened the scroll and found the passage where the prophet Isaiah (61:1–2a) is announcing his mission of liberation to the people of Zion. Taking those words for himself, Jesus and, by extension, the Holy Spirit proclaim their "mission manifesto" revealing the Spirit's liberationist priorities.[1] These priorities are concrete expressions of the socio-implicating spirituality that inspires the corporal works of mercy, Christian charity, liberation theology, Christian justice movements, and the Church's social teaching. "Spirituality is the great motivator. It is at the heart of theology and is behind the face that Christians reveal to their neighbors"[2] continually ever since the Spirit of Christ poured itself into the Church on the day of Pentecost.

In his Pentecost sermon (1978) entitled "Pentecost: Birth of the Church," El Salvadoran Archbishop and martyr Oscar Romero stressed that we Christians are a "new creation" and "we are responsible for the

---

* This chapter has undergone a number of transformations, beginning as my license thesis on the theme of liberation in the process of canonization for St. Clare in 1996. Cf. Cavazos-González, *Clara de Asís: Alter Christus*; "Liberation Spirituality," 142–52; "Five Pillars," 82. Most recently it was a talk presented as a Concurrent Session for the International Congress: "Transformed by Hope," on October 31, 2008, at Catholic Theological Union. It has been redacted, edited, and enlarged for this book.

1. Matthey, "Luke 4:16–30 The Spirit's Mission Manifesto," para. 2.

2. Cavazos-González, "Five Pillars," 82.

renovation of the world."[3] These words should cause us to tremble because as Spirit-filled believers we are called to the awesome responsibility of building God's Reign in this world. Every Pentecost, we pray that God will send his Holy Spirit to "renew the face of the earth"(Ps 104:30). The Holy Spirit will bring about this renewal by building God's Reign of justice, peace, and liberation with the collaboration of those who have been liberated by Christ. The Holy Spirit renews the world with and through the work of our hands as we live our Christian calling at home, at work, at church, and in society. This chapter will explain how this happens by touching upon two aspects of God's Reign. First, we will look at the presence of God's Reign as the Holy Spirit who invites the faithful to embrace their context through conversion. Secondly, we will focus on what I call the "five pillars of a liberating spirituality" as the way in which Christians as missionary disciples collaborate with God's Reign to renew the face of the earth.

GOD'S REIGN

The Christian Scriptures in Greek claim that Jesus preached the *basileia tou theou*. Often in English this is translated as God's kingdom or the kingdom of God as if it were only a place. *Basileia* is an abstract noun, best translated as sovereignty, kingship, or reign. Jesus's understanding of God's *basileia* was not so much about a place as it was God's act of reigning in people's lives. For this reason God's Reign is my preferred translation. It is both an action and a place.

CONVERSION TO GOD'S REIGN

When asked why he wanted to convene the Second Vatican Council, "Pope John XXIII said the time had come to open the windows [of the Church] and let in some fresh air."[4] Air is another translation for *ruah*, the Hebrew word for spirit. Since Vatican II the Holy Spirit has an importance in contemporary Christian theologies that is almost without precedence in Western spirituality. The Spirit of God is the animator of Christian spirituality, which begins with a personal encounter with Jesus Christ and the Reign of God.

3. Romero, "Pentecostés," section 2, para. 5. All translations of this and other Spanish sources are my own.

4. Sullivan, *101 Questions*, 17.

As I mentioned earlier in chapter 2, Christians participate in the liberating mission of Jesus by embracing reality. This is our *sequela Christi* (following Christ), which is the common call of all Christians. Through the *sequela* we are invited to conform our lives to his; to think and act in imitation of him. The *sequela Christi* is placing our feet into his footprints as we walk the road he walked in fulfillment of God's will. Walking in the footprints of Jesus translates into a profound commitment to the reality of God's Reign. This commitment begins with and is confirmed through conversion.

Conversion in the Christian Scriptures is called *metanoia,* which means a change in a person's way of thinking, which is to say, "a conscious process of changing one's behavior, world view, or self understanding."[5] This change takes place in the depths of a person's interior but is revealed in an external way through a change of direction and acceptance of God's kingship. The Scriptures also speak of conversion with the term *epistrepho,* meaning to turn around or return. The basic idea of Christian conversion is to turn one's back on sin, on evil, on a life without God and return to or to turn around and face God's sovereignty. Conversion as *metanoia* and *epistrepho* implies movement and not maintaining a "status quo."[6] This movement cannot be limited to an isolated moment because conversion is a gradual process taking the believer from an immature lifestyle to a mature and committed one.

Traditionally, this gradual process has been one of asceticism and penance (see sidebars). Unfortunately, limited understandings of penance and asceticism can lead people to focus in on their guilt and sinfulness and not on God's mercy and sanctification. While it is a good thing to acknowledge one's sin and fault, true penance and real asceticism are meant to help us see who we really are in all our good and bad, in our strength and weakness, with our

ASCETICISM

Asceticism comes from the Greek word *askesis*, which refers to the physical exercise needed to prepare one's self to compete in games like the ancient Olympics. Christians borrowed the word to speak of the exercise need to prepare oneself to run the race of salvation in Christ (1 Cor 9:24–27).

5. Warner, "Farm Workers," 69.

6. Cf. Galilea, *El seguimiento de Cristo,* 7–19; Moloney, "Conversion, I," 232–34; Lawrence, "Conversion, II," 234–38; Fragomeni, "Conversion," 231–32.

PENANCE

Penance or penitence comes from the Latin word *poene*, indicating a scarcity or lack that causes one pain or sorrow. Christianity uses the word to speak of what one does to show remorse for one's sin and to somehow, in one's limited way, respond to the question, "How can I repay the Lord for all the good done for me?" (Ps 116:12). Obviously we can never do enough, and God is satisfied with our simple act of trying.

virtues and vices. Penance is about turning to God and asceticism is the exercise needed to get in shape to join the pilgrim people of God as they walk in the footprints of Jesus. Penance is meant to help us look at ourselves as God sees us, and God sees us as beloved sons and daughters, coheirs with his only-begotten Son. It is true, God recognizes our faults and limitations, but above all God sees our gifts and potential. Often these need shaping and training. Ascetical practices are meant to strengthen us for the journey and, traditionally, these are spiritual exercises under three categories: fasting, prayer, and charity.

As I mentioned in chapter 1, Christians walk a triple way towards perfection, or rather one way with three efforts (purgation, illumination, and union). Here, I would like to focus a bit on the purgative effort or way. The purgative way is meant to purify and strengthen us through asceticism by helping us grow in the virtues of humility and obedience. These two virtues are also misunderstood by many Christians, and this misunderstanding hinders us along the way, often manifesting itself in the use of false humility and obedience. We need the help of the illuminative way to avoid misunderstanding the purgative way. As Christians we need to meditate on God's Word, the lives of the saints, and Church teaching in order to avoid misunderstanding this particular effort.

Humility is the virtue of unpretentiousness. Often, people understand humility as an admission of one's weaknesses and limitations. This is only one side of the coin. Humility also recognizes one's gifts and talents and puts these to use for the common good. For example, as a pastor, I often tried to get different parishioners involved in ministry or a parish project. Often, I would receive a response of false humility, with the person listing a variety of limitations. This was too bad, as it prevented the parishioner from sharing his or her talents with the rest of the parish. Perhaps by sharing his or her gifts, that parishioner could have made a difference in someone else's life, set an example for others, and grown in personal faith. False humility is a good way to keep from getting involved and taking responsibility. False humility keeps us from ever reaching union with God because it keeps us from union with God's people. The unitive effort requires us to have a clear understanding of humility (and obedience) as necessary for union with God and those whom God loves.

There is also a false obedience. Obedience is not asking "How high?" when an authority figure tells you to jump. Real obedience knows when to jump without being told to do so. The word *obedience* comes from the Latin *ab udire* (to hear). True obedience listens and responds to the needs of the Church, not just the hierarchy, and not excluding the hierarchy either. Obedience is not about compliance to the desires of the leadership of the Church or society but about responding to the real needs of God's people. This is not to deny the authority of a leader, because hopefully the needs of the people are discerned by the leader in conversation with them. The truly obedient Christian knows how to serve God's people, both cleric and lay. Often this obedient service takes the form of doing for others, but it should also include doing *with* others. Occasionally, the best service is no service at all. For example, good parents learn that the best way to serve their growing children is by letting them do things for themselves. Good parents also know how to take time away from familial duties and care for themselves whenever possible so they will not tire of caring for their sons and daughters. The truly obedient person also knows how to listen to his/her own needs and not burn the candle at both ends. The true servant knows when to work and when to rest in the process of renewing her/himself.

No one renews the world without first renewing him/herself. That is why Christ always calls us to conversion as an act of liberation. As a result, conversion has to be "a multi-dimensional (intellectual, affective, moral, religious, and socio-political) response to the love of God . . . [and] is expressed through the individual's decision to change one's relationship with the social world."[7] It is how we live our baptismal promise of renouncing sin through "liberation from egoism, from self-seeking, and from focus on one's own advantage."[8] In this way we liberate ourselves so to help liberate others. The Latin American bishops at Aperecida (2007) challenge the missionary disciples of Christ to "aid with preaching, catechesis, denun-

7. Warner, "Farm Workers," 69.

8. Hellmann, "Social Justice," 265.

ciation, and the testimony of love and justice"[9] in order to improve society and develop healthier social values. One's personal conversion should move in the direction of the social conversion implied by God's Reign.

This type of conversion presupposes the recognition of sin (both personal and social) and its consequences in our lives and in the world.[10] In facing sin we discover that it refuses to love and, as such, it resists God's Reign through malice, rejection, selfishness, or cowardly silence in the face of the misery of the poor. This is why conversion in Christian spirituality cannot simply be a private act; it demands a social dimension that relates it to the needs and aspirations of others, especially the poor, sick, and marginalized to which Jesus directed himself in a special way.[11] The call to conversion and purification on the part of every Christian and the whole Church is in favor of a preferential and evangelical option for the poor[12] and their integral liberation. Ongoing conversion will lead the Christian and the Church to identify themselves, as Francis (see sidebar) and Clare of Assisi and so many other saints have done, with the poor Christ and with our own poor. For these two saints and most Catholic saints, conversion

> ### St. Francis and the Leper
>
> As Francis's life drew to an end, he decided to write his testament. He began by remembering how he came to the Lord, which is to say, his process of conversion. Significant to his journey was the encounter he had with the leper.
>
> Francis who had always been frightened by lepers heard the leper's bell. But instead of running the other way, he faced the leper and saw him with God's eyes. Breaking with social convention, he was moved to embrace and kiss the leper. Francis wrote "that which was bitter became sweet". His life was changed forever.

9. CELAM, *Aparecida*, 385; Translation of this and other passages from the Aparecida Document are my own.

10. The Latin American bishops in Puebla are very clear in their affirmation that personal sin has social consequences that cause angst and frustration for a great many in the world. They especially condemn the growing gap between the rich and the poor as anti-Christian. Cf. CELAM, *Puebla*, 28, 73.

11. Cf. CELAM, *Puebla*, 1134, 1140; De Anasagasti, *Liberación en San Francisco de Asís,* 194–95.

12. The bishops at Aparecida tweaked the preferential option for the poor to be "the preferential and evangelical option for the poor," "making it clear that this is not merely a political or social position." Cf. Allen, "Bishops Draw," p. 1, para. 15.

is understood "as initiated by God and effected through serial social encounters charged with religious significance."[13] This type of conversion gives Christian spirituality a prophetic dimension that is "relentless in its struggle for justice."[14] In brief, every Christian conversion implies an interior change manifested in external acts of renewal, both personal and social, in order to collaborate with God's Reign.

COLLABORATING WITH GOD'S REIGN

Jesus's whole life and ministry had only one goal: the "impending dawn of the Reign of God."[15] He let himself be driven by the hope of this reign of liberation, peace, and justice. He was able to recognize it deep within humanity's historical reality as something that the passage of the centuries has not been able to stifle. Despite the harsh realities of social sin and injustice, the hope of the reality of God's Reign will not be extinguished. Jesus opens the eyes of his followers and friends to see the reality of God's Reign. He also teaches us that Christian spirituality calls his disciples to give of themselves and to deliver themselves in the practice of liberation. That is, to give life, and to give it to the fullest.

Oscar Romero, in a homily on Christian hope, invited the faithful to adopt a vigilant stance toward reality and to collaborate with God's Reign. He challenged us not to wait with crossed arms for God to establish peace, justice, and liberation, but rather to live in an active disposition of anticipation and cooperation.[16]

GOD'S COLLABORATOR

In the thirteenth century, the Franciscan Clare of Assisi wrote in a letter to Agnes of Prague that she considered her to be "someone who is God's collaborator and who supports the drooping limbs of his ineffable body." With this statement she very clearly identifies what it means to be God's collaborator. Collaboration with God implies taking care of the sick, the poor, the oppressed, and the marginalized.

---

13. Warner, "Farm Workers," 69.

14. Bowe, *Biblical Foundations of Spirituality*, 106.

15. Espín, "Mission of the Church," 884.

16. Cf. Romero, "Esperanza cristiana," last section, para. 2.

In this statement he reiterates what Christians like Paul of Tarsus, Clare of Assisi, Bartolome de las Casas, and Mother Teresa of Calcutta have stressed over the centuries: we are called to collaboration (see sidebar) and solidarity with God's Reign through concrete activity and ministry. This type of Christian solidarity and collaboration with God's Reign requires the pillars of contemplation, poverty, universal fraternity, Eucharist, and the cross.[17] These five pillars are how we express and strengthen a liberating Christian spiritual life. Let's look at each one individually.

CONTEMPLATIVE VISION

> If anyone says, "I love God," but hates his brother [or sister], he is a liar; for whoever does not love a brother [or sister] whom he has seen cannot love God whom he has not seen. This is the commandment we have from him: whoever loves God must also love his brother [and sister]. (1 John 4:20–21)

The first pillar of a liberating spirituality is a contemplative worldview. Only such a worldview can provide us with the intelligence, love, strength, and perseverance needed for the integral liberation God offers us.

The first step to any ministry of liberation needs to be prayer. Not a ritual formulistic type of prayer, but a liberating and transformative prayer that leads us to contemplation of the God we cannot see and to action on behalf of the brothers and sister whom we do see. Christian prayer teaches us to see God's power and action in all things and especially in life. Our Christian ancestors have always known this. As my colleague C. Vanessa White puts it, "Our grandmothers and grandfathers, our aunts and uncles—all our ancestors—testified to the power of God in their lives. Our sense of God is the basis and power of life."[18]

Prayer leads us to gratefully recognize and hope in God's *divina providencia* (divine providence), which is gracious presence and generosity. The experience of generosity through prayer helps us contemplate God as giver of life and as the one who calls us to an efficacy that does not fall into fatalism, but rises in the hope of the merciful and providential action of God in our lives and in history. This was the type of prayer that inspired the devout Catholic and founder of the United Farm Workers, César Chávez. He used to say, "Prayer is for you, for one's self. How do

17. Cavazos-González, "Liberation Spirituality," 142–52.
18. White, "Liturgy as a Liberating Force," 111.

you reach somebody through prayer who does not give a hoot about what you are doing? But prayer reaches you. Your prayer then translates into action and determination and faith."[19] This is truly contemplative prayer. Contemplation leads us to a full giving of ourselves to both God and neighbor.

Contemplation is self-oblation; it is the full giving of self. However, as Christians we realize that it is God who first gives himself to us. The experience of this reality requires that we be people of prayer. Prayer prepares and opens us up to experience God. Prayer helps us to encounter God and to be encountered by God. Prayer helps us respond to God's graciousness. Christian prayer is modeled on the prayer of María, who gave herself completely in response to God's Word in her life. In her prayer she pondered all the events of Jesus's life in her heart (Luke 2:19). But how exactly does one ponder?

> **CONTEMPLATION**
>
> In Christian spirituality contemplation is usually thought of as a passive or receptive type of prayer reached in the via unitiva. It is also traditionally described as a union with God. However, in a liberating Christian spirituality, contemplation is about union with God and those whom God loves.
>
> More than a passive vision of the divine, it is a way of looking at life, both human and divine, with and through God's eyes.

In my studies on Christian prayer, I find that we ponder in three ways: reflection, meditation, and contemplation. Reflection is basically a consideration of my life, my thoughts, my actions. As I pray, my prayer becomes a reflection of who I am and how I present myself to God. What I most often pray for says a lot about the type of person I am and what I hold dear. My prayer becomes a mirror in which I am reflected.

However, as Christians the mirror we are called to look into is not ourselves, but Jesus. When our prayer stops being about us, it becomes that of studying how we can be more Christ-like. It becomes meditation. And while reflection is the prayer of the purgative way, meditation is the prayer of the illuminative way. Meditation is our taking the time to ponder the life of Jesus as did María. It is entering into that life through an active imagination so that we can see ourselves in it. And as we gaze into the mirror that is Christ we take notice of the things in our life and

---

19. César Chávez, as quoted by Dalton, *Moral Vision of César Chávez*, 137.

our character that need to change to be strengthened so that we can be more in line with the Gospel.

Traditionally, reflection and meditation are thought of as very active types of pondering. They require our efforts and our prayer. Contemplation, on the other hand, is usually talked about as passive prayer and is the prayer of the unitive way. Contemplation is God's breaking through into our presence. It is God's manifesting himself to us, when and how God wants. In the face of God we can do little more than be open to God. Because it is the work of God, it requires our openness. God needs us to be actively receptive if we are to contemplate him.

Though passive in nature, contemplation should not be understood as something that is opposed to action. Contemplation and action need and enhance each other. Christian contemplation has to be apostolic, just as the apostolic dimension of Christian life needs to be contemplative in discerning "the mystery of God within the very heart of human engagement and contemplates the face of Christ in the faces of the brothers and sisters in need."[20] Contemplation and prayer inspire and give hope to any Christian action that is done in the service of the needy. Christian service and ministry animate and strengthen truly Christian prayer, devotion, and piety in the worship of God. Together contemplation and the apostolate form a contemplative vision.

A contemplative worldview helps us to see and recognize our neighbor as our brothers and sisters and to discover God in them, as did St. Martin of Tours (see sidebar). The least of our neighbors are the sacrament and mirror of the presence of Jesus; they are where the Son of God and María can be encoun-

> ## St. Martin of Tours
>
> You will often find images of St. Martin of Tours throughout Latin America. Normally, he is dressed as a Roman soldier sitting on a horse with a poor man at the feet of the horse. During the process of his conversion, Martin met a half-naked man in the dead of winter. Moved with pity, he sliced his cloak in half and gave half to the poor man.
>
> That same evening Jesus came to him in a dream and revealed that he had been the poor naked man on the road. He thanked Martin for his generosity.
>
> Martin abandoned his military duty and became a Christian dedicating his life to ministry and service of the poor.

20. Bowe, *Biblical Foundations of Spirituality*, 18–19.

tered. Contemplative vision not only helps us to encounter God in the neighbor, it also helps us to see our neighbor with the eyes of God and to see the other not just as an object of liberation but also as a sister and brother who accompanies us and whom we accompany toward an authentic liberation in the Spirit. Contemplative vision helps us appreciate the poor as a sacrament of Jesus, who for our "sake became poor" (2 Cor 8:9). Finally, a contemplative worldview helps us see ourselves as "pilgrims and strangers" in this world with a preferential and evangelical option for the poor and for poverty.

PREFERENTIAL AND EVANGELICAL OPTION FOR POVERTY

> For you know the gracious act of our Lord Jesus Christ, that for your sake he became poor although he was rich, so that by his poverty you might become rich (2 Cor 8:9)

Thanks to over a hundred years of Catholic social teaching, we have grown accustomed to speaking of the preferential option for the poor. It is at the center of the seven themes of the Church's social teaching[21] (see sidebar).

And it is nothing new. Concern for the poor has been a constant theme in Christian preaching and practice since Jesus identified himself with the poor. This siding with the poor on the part of Jesus has led many Christian saints to side with the poor themselves. Many have chosen to minister to the poor, while others have gone so far as to become poor themselves by abandoning a variety of careers to live and work more directly with the poor or by joining religious communities with a vow of poverty. Almost two thousand years of radical Gospel living on the part of many canonized saints and Christian movements challenges us to ongoing conversion and commitment to the poor through a preferential option for poverty. Conversion is not just a personal and moral act. It is more so a communitarian and social act that moves Christians beyond their own familiar world into the world of the poor in order to share in their way of living and their relationship with God and in this way assume and mirror the historical practice of Jesus of Nazareth. According to Oscar Romero, poverty is a Christian strength that forges the liberation of the people. To live in poverty as an evangelical virtue

21. USCCB, *Sharing Catholic Social Teaching*, section 4, para. 3–9.

demands a profound conversion that gives Christians the capacity to enter into the experience of the poor and simple (Matt 11:25). Francis, in his *Letter to All the Faithful*, and Clare of Assisi, in her *First Letter to Agnes*, remind us that Jesus, "although rich, made himself poor."[22] The Lord Jesus Christ abandoned himself completely to the ideal of poverty, to the point of dying "naked and poor" so we could learn that a liberating love is a *kenotic* love, which is not "self-centered, but one that finds its fulfillment in the giving of one's self for the benefit of others."[23]

I do not mean to glorify or romanticize poverty. The poor know all too well that poverty "means to die before one's time and to bury loved ones before their time."[24] Poverty kills. Latino theologian Roberto Goizueta reminds us that "poverty itself is not a value—indeed it is a *dis*-value and an evil."[25] Latin American liberation theologian Gustavo Gutiérrez called it a "subhuman situation."[26] This is precisely why the *kenosis* of Jesus is so powerful. In becoming poor and oppressed, Jesus, who knew no sin became sin, for our sakes (2 Cor 5:21) and died a violent death as a consequence. As a Christian virtue,

> **CATHOLIC SOCIAL TEACHING (USCCB)**
>
> 1. We believe in the sacred value of the *Life and Dignity* of the human person.
>
> 2. We are called to *Family, Community and Participation* in society's common good.
>
> 3. We need to protect every human being's *Rights and Responsibilities* to life and well-being.
>
> 4. Our Tradition calls us to make a *Preferential Option for the Poor and Vulnerable* (Matt 25:31–46).
>
> 5. We must protect the *Dignity of Work and the Rights of Workers* to participate in God's creation.
>
> 6. Our Gospel call to be peacemakers invites us to love all people and to enter into *Solidarity* with the diverse human family.
>
> 7. Our faith requires that we protect and *Care for God's Creation*.

---

22. 2 Corinthians 8:9, as quoted by Francis and Clare of Assisi; cf. *EpFid* 5, and 1 *EpAgn* 17–24

23. Sobrino, *Liberación con Espíritu*, 45.

24. César Chávez, as quoted by Dalton, *Moral Vision of César Chávez*, 119.

25. Goizueta, "Christology of Jon Sobrino," 96.

26. Gutiérrez, *Theology of Liberation*, 164.

religious vow, and evangelical counsel, poverty is still recognized as a social evil and yet is paradoxically embraced in order to live liberation in the "ex-centricity of love to the point of the radical abandonment of one's self."[27] Fidelity to what Francis of Assisi called "most high poverty" is, in reality, being united to Jesus, who loves the poor "who cannot take life for granted."[28]

Jesus himself embraced poverty as a way of life. Augustine of Hippo recalls, "Christ is at once rich and poor: as God, rich; as a human person, poor. Truly, that Man rose to heaven already rich, and now sits at the right hand of the Father, but here, among us, he still suffers hunger, thirst and nakedness: here he is poor and is in the poor."[29] This is the Son of God we follow, the one who called himself Son of Man.

The *sequela* of the poor, naked, and crucified Jesus is rooted in the experience of a "friendly" *encuentro* with the Lord himself (John 15:15) in the service of others, especially the poor. The presence of the poor and impoverished opens our eyes to the reality that God's creation is threatened, stained, and in need of being liberated from sin and healed of its consequences. Their presence also can lead us to ask questions about the existing relationship between humanity and creation. In the voice of the poor, the infirm, the alternately documented immigrant, the rejected, the oppressed, and even in the voice of the ravished earth the groans of the Holy Spirit can be heard as s/he intercedes for us (Rom 8:26).

Christians walking in the freedom of the children of God are motivated by the Spirit of love to be in solidarity and communion with all of creation, with all of humanity, and in a special way with the poor, naked, and crucified people of the world and even the planet itself (see sidebar).[30] They embrace poverty "not for the sake of poverty, but for the sake of resisting injustice and for the sake of working with the poor to liberate themselves from their unjust suffering."[31]

Christians do not shy away from the evil poverty. Rather, they opt to face it head on in order to liberate its victims. In opting to deal with poverty and serve the poor, Christians need to be directed by the Holy

---

27. Sobrino, *Liberación con Espíritu*, 45.

28. Goizueta, "Christology of Jon Sobrino," 96; cf. Iriarte, *Vocación*, 180–85.

29. Augustine of Hippo, Sermon 123,4, as quoted in Augustinians, "Preferential Option," last para.

30. Katoppo, "Poor Mother Earth."

31. Dalton, *Moral Vision of César Chávez*, 101.

Spirit so that their acts of liberation will not lead to new forms of slavery. Acts of charity done for the benefit of the poor and needy will be motivated by a sense of mutuality and respect for the poor as sisters and brothers in the human *familia*. This type of solidarity goes beyond the scope of social concern; it is the desire of transforming creation into the universal brotherhood and sisterhood of God's Reign.

UNIVERSAL BROTHERHOOD AND SISTERHOOD

For all of you who were baptized into Christ have clothed yourselves with Christ. There is neither Jew nor Greek, there is neither slave nor free person, there is not male and female; for you are all one in Christ Jesus. And if you belong to Christ, then you are Abraham's descendant, heirs according to the promise. (Gal 3:27–29)

> **POOR MOTHER EARTH**
>
> The largest English newspaper in Indonesia, The Jakarta Post, published an article entitled "Poor Mother Earth, Your Children Treat You Like Dirt," by Marianne Katoppo. The article's evocative title bemoaned the fact that the earth is being ravished by materialism and the pollution and garbage it produces. Sadly, human greed has turned the rich earth into a poor mother who can barely sustain all her children.

The third pillar of liberating spirituality is universal brotherhood and sisterhood within a context of hope. Hope is essential to living a Christian life. Along with faith and love it is one of the three theological virtues that keep us strong in the face of adversity. Christian hope is focused on Jesus Christ present among the poor and impoverished and helps us live what Gustavo Gutiérrez calls "spiritual infancy,"[32] which is a hopeful attitude of openness and humble availability to God in spiritual poverty. It is "marked by a profound sense of our own creatureliness, knowing who we are before God with our finitude and human limitations."[33] Hope is also faith in the Son of Man who in his *kenosis* performed liberation miracles for and in solidarity with his brothers and sisters, the poor and

---

32. Gustavo Gutiérrez calls this *infancia spiritual*, which can also be translated as "spiritual childhood." "The Bible calls this attitude [of the humility needed to work with the poor] 'spiritual infancy,' which Gutiérrez defines as an 'attitude of openness to God, an attitude of the availability of one who looks to the Lord of all things'" (Sobrino, *Spirituality of Liberation*, 57).

33. Bowe, *Biblical Foundations of Spirituality*, 178.

marginalized. This solidarity with the least of his brothers and sisters led Jesus to share their suffering to the point of trial, crucifixion, and death.

"Therefore," Latino theologian Orlando Espín boldly proclaims, "a Christian must be first and foremost a person committed to solidarity with suffering victims (like Jesus). And this commitment must be brought to bear in every aspect of daily life, both private and public."[34] For example, Christians choose to accompany the least and many even live a life of poverty as a way of rejecting and challenging the social evil of poverty. In this way, like Jesus, they accompany the poor in solidarity and communion, but always with hope in God's Reign, which encompasses much more than a socio-economic liberation. We cannot afford to look at the world of those in need just as a place of ministry or social service. We Christians need to see it as a place of residence. It is a school of Christian solidarity (see sidebar) where one learns to feel, reason, make friends, believe, suffer, and celebrate with the poor.

While the preferential and evangelical option for the poor may seem to canonize the poor and villainize the wealthy, Christians can never forget that we are *all* brothers and sisters. Human life must be recognized and respected in *all* people. Christ-centered liberation is for *all* people. The liberation of women and men, poor and rich, people of color and white people, the infirm and the healthy, of the oppressed and of the oppressors, must be an integral liberation that leads to an under-

34. Espín, *Faith of the People*, 28.

standing of life based on the concepts of sisterhood, brotherhood, and communion.

Often people who are oppressed or who labor in solidarity with the poor, the social outcasts, and otherwise marginalized people cannot find it in their hearts to forgive the rich and those who oppress the downtrodden. They are all too familiar with the hurt and destruction that has been heaped upon the downtrodden over the centuries and still is. How can we look at our enemy and love him or her? African American theologian Diana Hayes invites us not to become like them, but rather she insists that

> we need to teach them to be open to a more holistic, inclusive and communitarian way of living and working in the world. Rather than competition and individual success at the expense of others, we should be seeking to develop avenues of communication and paths of dialogue that will enrich us all, not just a few. Such a mode of being in the world would certainly be more in keeping with the true model of church given to us by Jesus in his mission and ministry of love, compassion and community.[35]

The Christian belief in God is based on the God of love, compassion, and community that we call the Most Holy Trinity. God is a communion or, better yet, a *familia* that we call Father (or Mother), Child, and Holy Spirit. Like Latino and other traditional socio-centered *familias*, God is a family of ever-widening circles of relationships. Hispanic families are forever welcoming friends and acquaintances to become part of the *familia*. So too does God. We are Christians because we are incorporated into God's household in baptism, and this makes us all male and female, rich and poor (see sidebar), oppressed and oppressors, members of the same *familia*.[36] This *familia*, however, cannot limit itself to the baptized. "Spiritual infancy" necessarily leads to a spiritual sisterhood and brotherhood that excludes no one. The spiritual journey cannot be walked alone. It requires our walking as a *familia* united in God. Following Jesus according to the Spirit motivates Christians to break with self-serving and ego-centered individualism so that they can commit to collaborate and coexist with others, be they poor or rich, victims or victimizers. In this way, all Christian life is Eucharistic. Like the bread and wine at the offertory rite of the Mass, all Christian life is offered for the greater

35. D. Hayes, "To Be the Bridge," 69.
36. Cf. Romero, "Por su alianza."

Who Are the Poor?

I have purposely chosen to focus on the economically and materially poor in this section. But rest assured, there are all sorts of "poor people."

A Mexican proverb states *Los ricos tambien lloran* ("The rich also cry"). In Spanish it is not uncommon to use the word *pobrecito* ("little poor one") when showing sympathy for someone who is having a difficult time for whatever reason. Even in English we often hear poor used before someone's name to express that the person is having a rough time.

The poor are those who are missing the basic necessities of a full life: food, clothing, housing, work, education, family, friends, health, and happiness. A Christian preferential option for the poor highlights service of the materially poor without neglecting those who are poor in other ways.

honor and glory of God, for our good and for the good of *all* our sisters and brothers, not just the Church.

EUCHARISTIC COMMUNION

For as often as you eat this bread and drink the cup, you proclaim the death of the Lord until he comes. Therefore whoever eats the bread or drinks the cup of the Lord unworthily will have to answer for the body and blood of the Lord. (1 Cor 11:24–27)

The Christian calling in the world is lived in a spirituality of grateful communion. For Catholics, the word *communion* always brings to mind the image of the Eucharist, and rightly so. The Eucharist left to us by Jesus is our communion with him and with his body. It brings the wide variety of Christians from around the world together like different kinds of grain into one multigrain loaf of bread (see sidebar). "Because the loaf of bread is one, we, though many, are one body, for we all partake of the one loaf" (1 Cor 10:17).

Pope Benedict XVI reminds us that "in sacramental communion I become one with the Lord, like all the other communicants."[37] In this way all the communicants enter into communion not just with the Lord but with each other. Communion with the body and blood of the Lord also commits Christians to a communion with all persons and in particular with the poorest ones. In the Eucharist, love of God, love of the Church, and love of neighbor become one.

37. Benedict XVI, *Deus caritas est*, 14.

A spirituality of communion makes the Eucharist apt nourishment for those who want to truly live a liberating spirituality. Such a spirituality does not shy away from sacrifice, though. Sacrifice is not something we like to do. It is difficult and frustrating to give one's life for the cause of liberation. U.S. American heroes like Martin Luther King and César Chávez knew this firsthand; they gave their lives for the noble cause of human dignity.

Sacrifice and commitment are essential to the work of liberation. Like Jesus, Martin Luther King knew that "every step toward the goal of justice requires sacrifice, suffering, and struggle; the tireless exertions and passionate concern of dedicated individuals."[38] César Chávez also knew the spiritual power of *la lucha* (struggle) and sacrifice. He invited us to recognize, "once people are willing to make sacrifices, you develop a power of spirit which can affect your adversaries in way [sic] you can hardly imagine."[39]

> **MULTIGRAIN BREAD**
>
> In my travels I have had the opportunity to celebrate Mass with a wide variety of people. But I don't need to go far to see the variety of grains found in the bread that we call the body of Christ. Not too long ago, I was at Mass in Chicago's Holy Name Cathedral. As I knelt for the consecration I saw before me a vast array of people. My eyes focused on a homeless man who knelt close to a well-to-do woman. I smiled at that Eucharistic vision of communion and prayed it would move from the pews to the streets as the multigrain bread we call Church takes the Gospel into the world.

Jesus also knew the power of sacrifice, which is why he established the Eucharist within the context of his passion, death, and resurrection. On the night before he died he broke the bread and blessed the wine, asking, "Do this in memory of me." In his encyclical letter on love, Pope Benedict explains how Jesus gave his "act of oblation an enduring presence through his institution of the Eucharist at the Last Supper. He anticipated his death and resurrection by giving his disciples, in the bread and wine, his very self, his body, and blood as the new manna."[40] The painful context of the passion, death, and resurrection of Jesus Christ gives the Eucharist a significance of sacrifice for the cause of the integral

---

38. Martin Luther King Jr. as quoted by Nolan, "Introductory Remarks," para. 3.

39. César Chávez, as quoted by Dalton, *Moral Vision of César Chávez*, 83.

40. Benedict XVI, *Deus caritas est*, 13.

liberation of all people, and it was the way in which Jesus wished to establish his presence among his community as a memorial of his life and work.[41]

For all Christians, the Eucharist is the commemoration of Jesus's life, ministry, and ongoing presence. Most mainline Christian denominations also share in the belief that Jesus is somehow present in, with or through the Eucharistic bread and wine. For Roman Catholics and Orthodox Christians it is a Sacrament and the "real presence" of Jesus in and for the world. St. Alphonse Ligouri reminds us that in the Eucharist Jesus is truly present and remains with humankind out of love.[42] It is how Jesus is with his followers till the end of time. Christ's real presence continues the *kenosis* and poverty of Jesus who, in this Sacrament, opens himself to the faithful and his enemies as well. In the Eucharist, Jesus is worshipped and adored by his followers, scorned and rejected by those who hate him and his Church.

Alphonse Ligouri claimed, "Love makes the lover like the beloved."[43] In receiving the Sacrament of the Eucharist Sunday after Sunday, let us pray that we become what we eat and drink. We encounter the real presence of Christ in the Eucharist so that in us the world can encounter the real presence of Christ who liberates all people from sin and helps them overcome its consequences. What we receive at communion, we must live in our homes, work, politics, charity, and play. This demands our living in communion with others and sacrificing for the cause of liberation. In this way we become like our beloved Jesus; we become more and more the real presence of Christ in the world.

Besides being real presence, sacrifice, and communion, Eucharist is also thanksgiving and gratitude, two things that those who work for liberation cannot be without. Jesus took the bread and gave thanks. Then he took the cup and again gave thanks. His whole life was praise and thanksgiving to God, his loving *Abba*. So on the night before he died, he gave thanks and praise in the breaking of the bread and the sharing of the cup. This simple meal of bread and wine became for us the Eucharist, a memorial of our Lord's passion, death, and resurrection. Jesus gave the Eucharist an importance without equal, because it was for him an act of thanksgiving that cannot be repeated, because life can only be given up once. We,

41. Cf. Balasuriya, *Eucharist and Human Liberation*, 16.

42. Alphonse Ligouri, "To Jesus in the Blessed Sacrament," para. 1.

43. Alphonse Ligouri, "Practice of the Love of Jesus," 126.

however, offer it over and over again in memory of his singular sacrifice. The Eucharist given to us by Jesus is intimately united to real presence, to thanksgiving, to the communion of persons, to bread broken and wine shared, and to the pain and liberating sacrifice of the cross.

THE SIGN OF THE CROSS

> For Christ did not send me to baptize but to preach the gospel, and not with the wisdom of human eloquence, so that the cross of Christ might not be emptied of its meaning. The message of the cross is foolishness to those who are perishing, but to us who are being saved it is the power of God. (1 Cor 1:17–18)

The final pillar of a liberating Christian spirituality is the sign of the cross. Spirituality cannot be Christian without the cross of Jesus Christ. In this sign we are invited to conquer personal and social sin to liberate and heal each other from the consequences of that sin. The Christian Scriptures teach us that ours is a spirituality whose foundation is the cross of our Lord Jesus Christ. His is not an empty cross, because for as long as people suffer at the hands of others and are in need of some kind of liberation, Jesus remains crucified. He "experiences the full ravages of our human condition, not only by undergoing death, but by undergoing an unjust, violent death."[44] We are called to this mystery.

In baptism we enter into the paschal mystery and receive the liberating sign of the cross as our calling card; the symbol of our incorporation into the death and resurrection of Jesus Christ so that we can follow him on the road to a new life (Rom 6:4). "To live in solidarity with the crucified Christ is to abide in his life-giving Spirit."[45] The *sequela* of Jesus requires the cross as both solidarity and sacrifice so as to become life-givers. The cross involves us in its contemplation; it leaves us bare; it leaves us at the feet of Jesus and reveals him in the least of our brothers and sisters, especially those who are crucified in the *lucha* (effort, fight) for liberation in today's world. It calls us to give them life and liberty. It is our sign of service and the primary symbol of our faith.

Over the course of two thousand years we have seen the cross and the crucifix transformed into marvelous and inspiring works of art (see sidebar). We find images of the cross and crucifixion in our churches and homes. Many of us as Christians wear the symbol of the cross or

44. Goizueta, "Christology of Jon Sobrino," 99.

45. Diaz, "Life-Giving Migrations," para. 33.

The Cross in Christian Art

The image of the cross and the crucified savior has undergone several transformations in Christian art over the centuries. These variations have had to do with our Christian understanding of Jesus. In the first Christian millennium the primary image of Jesus crucified was that of the royal or priestly Savior standing upright and majestically over the cross. The cross was the throne that he reigned from. All vestiges of the horror of the cross were wiped clean in the glory of the resurrection.

From the thirteenth century on, the Church—wanting to stress the humanity of Christ—began to have artists depict Jesus bent and sagging on the cross. As time went on, artists laid upon his image all the horrors of the passion and the agony of death. His image called out for compassion as many Christians moved to do the corporal works of mercy, helping the poor and impoverished, to ease the pain of Jesus, who sided with the suffering people of the world.

From the sixteenth century, some Christians began to insist on a body-less image of the cross or no cross at all. Their desire to focus on the resurrection is a crucifix hanging from our necks. The bloodiness of the wood, however, has been replaced by the glint of gold and silver in a symbol that we much too often try to domesticate. We should never forget that the symbol of the cross, which we love and kiss, was born in violence and agony. It took shape in the heart of the Christian community as Jesus's mother, María, and a few disciples watched him suffer and die upon an ugly wooden cross on a Good Friday many centuries ago. It calls out to us in its horror.

The Latin American bishops united at the fifth General Conference of the Latin American and Caribbean Episcopates in Aparecida (2007) teach us that, "Enlightened by Christ, suffering, injustice and the cross call us to live as a Samaritan Church (cf. Luke 10:25–37), mindful that 'evangelization has always been tied to human promotion and authentic Christian liberation.'"[46] This is the sign of the cross that empowers us to take up our cross every day and follow Jesus so that where he is there we might be. Like the Good Samaritan, Jesus is with the poor and impoverished; he is taking up their crosses and easing their burdens. That is where the cross and the other four pillars of liberating spirituality call us to be.

46. CELAM, *Aparecida*, 26.

The way of conversion that is expressed in a contemplative world-view, in a life of poverty, in universal sisterhood and brotherhood, and celebrated in a Eucharistic communion must take very seriously the "sign of the cross." With the horror of the cross present in our minds, we Christians need to insist that the scandal and folly of the cross are the strength and the wisdom of God. This is why "we proclaim Christ crucified" (1 Cor 1:23). Without the sacrifice of the cross in our *cotidiano* there is no salvation, no liberation, no conversion, and no Christianity.

(cont.) understandable. Still the cross, with or without a corpus, cannot be denied. The continued suffering and death of Jesus in the poor, the hungry, the naked, the homeless, the infirm, the imprisoned, the oppressed, and other suffering people cannot be denied either.

IN CONCLUSION

Christian Spirituality is not only self-implicating, it is socio-implicating; it is a liberating spirituality. Such spirituality challenges us to walk in the liberating Spirit of Jesus Christ, not just to renew ourselves but to renew the world. Reflecting with the poor and the impoverished on the life of Jesus of Nazareth, every Christian is invited to an *encuentro* with the living and life-giving Jesus with and in the marginalized so as to participate in the liberation that he offers through conversion and renewal. This is a continuous process of liberation from sin, from injustice, from death, and from the barriers that separate us. Christian liberation is one that is open to the personal and social liberation of all, rich and poor, oppressor and oppressed alike. It is a transcendent liberation that cannot be limited exclusively to a socio-political liberation. It looks to penetrate all aspects of the "socio-spiritual"[47] life of the human person and all humanity with God's Reign.

Walking in the Spirit and collaborating with the Reign of God is founded on the example of Jesus Christ, who denied himself in order to give himself completely to the reality of his context. Like Jesus, we Christians need to respect the historical reality of our own contexts. We

47. By "socio-spiritual" I understand all of the aspects of the human life. "Socio" = social, political, religious, economic, and material; in other words, the exterior life. "Spiritual" = spiritual, educational, cultural, affective and psychological; in other words, the interior life.

are faithful to that reality by responding to its demands with God's Reign. Like our brothers and sisters across two millennia, we are called to announce good news to the poor, liberate the captives, challenge oppressors, and invite all people to conversion through the sign of the cross.

DISCUSSING CHAPTER 5

Questions about the Material

What are *metanoia* and *epistrepho*?

What is true obedience?

How do we collaborate with God's Reign?

How do we define the five pillars?

Questions about Your Own Experience

How do you develop your own contemplative worldview?

What steps are you taking to make a preferential option for poverty?

Whom do you find difficult (or easy) to accept as brothers and sisters in the Lord?

How do you build Eucharistic communion?

What does the sign of the cross mean in your life?

Conclusion

Christian Aspiration

THERE CAN BE NO Christian spiritual life, no Christian spiritual formation or a Christian liberating spirituality without the Holy Spirit. Therefore, as we come to the end of this book, I would like to highlight the presence of God's Spirit in the life of the Church and each individual Christian. Jesus himself highlights the importance of the Spirit:

> Jesus answered, "Amen, amen, I say to you, no one can enter God's Reign without being born of water and Spirit. What is born of flesh is flesh and what is born of spirit is spirit. Do not be amazed that I told you, 'You must be born from above.' The wind blows where it will, and you can hear the sound it makes, but you do not know where it comes from or where it goes; so it is with everyone who is born of the Spirit." (John 3:5–8)

Jesus's description of the Spirit and those born of the Spirit are likened to the wind in all its freedom. The wind is free to blow and move where it will. The freedom of the wind and therefore of the Spirit is very liberating. In addition, for those of us who have been "born of water and the Spirit," Christian spirituality is meant to be liberating.

I like to talk about the Christian calling in terms of "liberating spirituality." This is meant to be a double entendre, which is to say, it has a double meaning. It is a reference to Christian spirituality as liberating. At the same time it is an invitation to liberate spirituality from those who relegate it to Church on Sunday, new age self-help, occult superstition, or fundamentalist aggression. The title of this book on liberating spirituality is "Beyond Piety" but it is not a negation of piety or devotional practice (see sidebars). We need our candles, rosaries, Bible studies, novenas, prayer meetings, and other practices that help educate and strengthen

---

PIETY

Piety is the virtue of reverence for God and righteous behavior. In Christianity the pious are stereotypically people who practice traditional spiritual exercises like the rosary, Bible study, singing hymns, and the like.

---

our affection for and commitment to God and God's people. Personally, I love pious and devotional practice. I wear a crucifix and a rosary ring. My office is filled with statues of Jesus, María, and various *santos* and *santas*. I still like to light candles and bless myself every time I drive by a Catholic Church. However, I also know that it does me no good to wear a crucifix if I do nothing for the crucified people of the earth. I should not kiss an image of Jesus, María, or the saints if I am not willing to act like them. Lighting a candle means nothing without the light of charity, and blessing myself is empty ritual if I do not practice justice, work for peace, and lend a hand to liberate the poor and oppressed. The U.S. bishops remind us that pious and devotional practices need to have a social character, reminding us that the Gospel has a definite social dimension. "God has created us as social beings by our very nature. We always live in a relationship of interdependence with others and always have a responsibility to work for the common good of our society."[1]

DEVOTION

Devotion is another way to talk about piety. However, it moves piety into the realm of affection, enthusiasm, and commitment. Traditionally devotion is tied to practices like the Stations of the Cross, prayer to the Sacred Heart of Jesus, wearing the scapular, and other prayerful practices.

LIBERATED IN CHRIST

Traditionally, Christian spirituality liberates believers from sin and empowers them to triumph over its consequences so that once liberated, Christians will work to liberate others. As liberated people we are free from the guilt and shame of past sins; we are free or are becoming free of things that keep us from living life to our full potential and from reaching out to other people. Liberated Christians are not necessarily free of the worries, concerns, or problems found in the *cotidiano*. We are, however, graced with the fruits of the Spirit so that hope will keep us filled with the peace and joy that no one can take from us, *gracias*

---

1. USCCB, *Popular Devotional Practices*, 12.

a Dios (thanks be to God: see sidebar). Liberated Christians are not necessarily free to do whatever we please. On the contrary, we are liberated from disordered needs, selfish desires, and ego-centrism so that we can freely love our family, friends, and enemies, serve our neighbor, and assist the poor and downtrodden. As people liberated by the life, death, and resurrection of Jesus, we are gifted with the Spirit and called to live the Gospel message of Christ. We are liberated like Jesus, to bring good news to the poor, liberty to the captives, recovery of sight to the blind, and freedom to the oppressed. As Catholic, Orthodox, Protestant, Evangelical and nondenominational, we Christians belong to a religion that has a long tradition of caring for the poor.

A RELIGIOUS WAY OF LIFE

Ours is a two-thousand-year-old religion, even though some Christians claim that Christianity is not a religion but a way of life. They are partially correct. Christianity is a religion, and all religions are ways of life. Christianity is a religious way of life founded on the rock of Jesus's experience of God as *Abba* and being called to build God's Reign in the world. This experience was and is a religious one, but it is also a political, social, and economic experience. Ultimately, it is a spiritual experience because it deals with the whole person and the whole world.

As Christians we are not of this world, yet we are intimately tied to it because we are called to live out our Christian vocation in the world. Like Jesus and the Spirit, when it comes to our presence in this world we are pilgrims and *inmigrantes* in a foreign land. We are "alternately

> ### GRACIAS A DIOS
>
> I have often experienced for myself the peace and joy that no one or nothing can take from us. I've had those fruits for a long time, but it wasn't till my friend Felix pointed it out that I took notice.
>
> It was my last year in priestly studies and I was going crazy trying to finish all my homework, get my ordination planned, and manage a slight crisis in vocational discernment. I had just lost a final paper to a computer glitch when Felix called. As I was listing my woes, he laughed. I was caught off guard at his laughter and had to smile to myself. It was then that he told me that he wanted to know why despite everything I still had a serenity that he found envious. "Gracias a Dios" ("Thanks to God") was my immediate response. I believed it then and I believe it still.

FORGIVE US LORD!

While many Christians have spent their lives helping the poor and working to liberate the captives, many others have done just the opposite. As a Church (Catholic, Orthodox, Protestant, evangelical, and nondenominational) we have done our share of oppressing people and leaving them in poverty. We have been responsible for the excommunication of "alternative believers" (heretics), the Crusades, the Inquisition, the burning of "witches," and the destruction of various native cultures in America and elsewhere, the political stands that keep people poor, and other fundamentalist type attacks at people "who are not like us."

Therefore, let us learn from our mistakes and let us pray to God for forgiveness and commit ourselves as individual believers and whole churches to the liberating mission of Jesus Christ. (Luke 4:18–19)

documented."[2] Our papers are the waters of baptism that join us together as the Church built by Jesus and his original disciples. In baptism our sins are forgiven, and we are born again as adopted sons and daughters of God: "a member of Christ and a temple of the Holy Spirit. By this very fact the person baptized is incorporated into the Church, the Body of Christ, and made a sharer in the priesthood of Christ"(*CCC* 1279). As sharers in Jesus Christ, who is the priest, prophet, and king, we live a religious way of life that is centered on a reign that is not of this world. Nonetheless, we walk in solidarity with this world that Jesus came to save and liberate (John 18:36). It is here on earth and not "over there" in heaven where we live our Christian calling. Our spiritual lives are carried out on an earth that needs salvation, with people who need liberation. We ourselves, in body, soul and spirit, share in the same need for salvation and liberation. We are called to live and grow in the "glorious freedom of the children of God" and to share that freedom with a creation that groans for its own liberation (Rom 8:19–24).

---

2. Nanko-Fernández, "From Pajaro to Paraclete," para. 40.

GROWING AS CHRISTIANS

Thanks be to God we do not have to do this alone. While Jesus has returned to the homeland, his Spirit continues marching with us, walking with us, crossing borders and breaking down walls with us. We and the Holy Spirit continue the presence of Jesus in this world. Together with María, the saints, and the Church, each one of us belongs to a *familia* of Spirit-filled believers that do the will of the Father and extend Jesus and his mission through time and space on this earth. This *familia* or household of God helps and challenges us to grow in our liberating identity as Christians.

The varied Word of God also helps us on our journey. When we read God's Word in the Sacred Scriptures, the lives of the saints, and Church teaching, we discover that Jesus came to free the oppressed and set the captives free. His mother sang of a day when the hungry would be well fed and the rich sent away empty handed. His disciples have reached out to the poor and oppressed over the course of two thousand years in many and varied ways. Sadly, we have also done our share of wrong and made mistakes along the way (see previous page). These are the stories (the good and the bad) that need to inform our way of life, our religion, our spirituality. We find them not just in the Bible but everywhere that God's living Word abides: Scripture, Creation, and History.

As Christians we are called to read the books of God's Word not just for the practice of lectio divina but in order to reenvision our lives as true disciples of Christ. In so doing we are invited by the Church and the Spirit to a Christian spirituality of liberation. The following are the ways in which we can express and strengthen our spirituality and grow as Christians:

1. *Prayer and a Contemplative Worldview.* A lot of people who work to liberate others but have no prayer life tend to burn out and give up. On the other hand, many people who spend all their time in prayer and spiritual reading do not see beyond their own salvation and often close their eyes to the world around them. A liberating spirituality fosters pious devotion as the way to a contemplative worldview that will open our eyes to the presence of God in all and to the needs of the poor and downtrodden.

2. *Personal Conversion and Universal Sister/Brotherhood.* With our contemplative eyes wide open we see our sins and ask God and neighbor for forgiveness. We also see our neighbors—all our

neighbors—as brothers and sisters, sons and daughters of one God. This necessarily calls us to personal conversion, meaning we adjust our lives to better serve God and neighbor in whatever Christian denomination we find ourselves.

3. *Preferential Option for Poverty and Ministry.* The universal brother/sisterhood of God's *familia* invites all Christians to ministry. For Christians, ministry is not just about worship and Church service. More and more it is crucial that ministry be the Christian way of reaching out to the world around us and to service of the poor. In so doing, spiritual poverty becomes a humble and simple way of life chosen to eradicate material poverty.

4. *Worship and Eucharistic Communion.* As the poor of Christ we are called to a life of *kenosis. Kenosis* is self-abnegation or learning how to deny ourselves for the good of others. It is in this practice of self-denial that our worship and devotional practices take on real meaning. Only those who are emptying themselves can truly be filled with the Eucharistic communion that is Christ and his body, the Church.

5. *Witnessing to the Sign of the Cross.* As Christians we are sealed with the cross of Jesus Christ. Without denying the agony and horror of the cross, we affirm its power to save because of the blood of Christ. The blood that he poured out on that cross liberates us, so that we in turn will carry his cross, which is the cross of the poor and downtrodden of this world.

I began this book with the sound of the wind; the sound of the Spirit. As Christians we are a People born of the Spirit. Individually, we are the rustling leaves, strong buildings, crashing waters, tranquil meadows, and majestic hills where the wind of the Spirit becomes a song, a whistle, a whisper, or a moan; where the human spirit proclaims *"I have been crucified with Christ, yet I live, no longer I, but Christ who lives in me"* (Gal 2:20).

Our most Christian aspiration is to have the same attitude of Christ (Phil 2:5). As Paul reminds us in the letter to the Galatians (3:27), those of us who have been baptized in Christ have died to sin and selfishness and have been clothed in Christ. We have put him on, so that those who see us see Jesus. And so we allow Christ to spread his message to the poor and to the world with our mouths, to touch and heal the sick with our hands, to march against oppression and injustice with our feet, to liberate and release the captives with our lives.

Bibliography

Allen, Jr., John L. "Bishops Draw on Legacy of Liberation Theology." *National Catholic Reporter*, June 8, 2007, 1–3. Online: http://findarticles.com/p/articles/mi_m1141 / is_29_43/ai_n27284244/.

Alphonse Ligouri. "The Practice of the Love of Jesus." In *Alphonsus de Ligouri: Selected Writings*, edited by Frederick M. Jones. Classics of Western Spirituality. Mahwah, NJ: Paulist Press 1999.

——. "To Jesus in the Blessed Sacrament." The Work of God: Holy Eucharist, Eucharistic Prayers. No pages. Online: http://www.theworkofgod.org/Prayers /eucharist_prayers.asp?key=6.

Ashley, J. Matthew. "The Mystery of God and Compassion for the Poor: The Spiritual Basis of Theology." In *Hope and Solidarity: Jon Sobrino's Challenge to Christian Theology*, edited by Stephen J. Pope, 63–75. Maryknoll, NY: Orbis Books, 2008.

Augustinians of the Midwest. "The Preferential Option for the Poor: Reflections from St. Augustine." Adapted from the International Augustinian Secretariate for Justice and Peace Bulletin. No pages. Online: http://www.midwestaugustinians.org /justpaxprefopt_aug.html.

Balasuriya, Tissa. *The Eucharist and Human Liberation*. Maryknoll, NY: Orbis Books, 1980.

Bauer, Judith A. *The Essential Mary Handbook: A Summary of Beliefs, Devotions and Prayers*. Ligouri MO: Ligouri Publications, 1999.

Benedict XVI. *Deus caritas est*. Vatican Papal Archive. Libreria Editrice Vaticana, 2005. No pages. Online: http://www.vatican.va/holy_father/benedict_xvi/encyclicals /documents/hf_ben-xvi_enc_20051225_deus-caritas-est_en.html.

——. *Spe salvi*. Vatican Papal Archive. Libreria Editrice Vaticana, 2007. No pages. Online: http://www.vatican.va/holy_father/benedict_xvi/encyclicals/documents /hf_ben-xvi_enc_20071130_spe-salvi _en.html.

Bevans, Stephan B. *Models of Contextual Theology*. Revised and expanded ed. Faith and Cultures. Maryknoll, NY: Orbis Books, 2002.

Bowe, Barbara E. *Biblical Foundations of Spirituality: Touching a Finger to the Flame*. Lanham, MD: Rowman & Littlefield, 2003.

Browning, W. R. F. "Son of Man." In *A Dictionary of the Bible*. (1997). Online: http: //www. encyclopedia.com/doc/1O94-SonofMan.html.

Burke, Kevin F., and Robert Lassalle-Klein, *Love that Produces Hope: The Thought of Ignacio Ellacuria*. Collegeville, MN: Liturgical Press, 2006.

Byrne, Richard. "Journey (Growth and Development in Spiritual Life)." In *New Dictionary of Catholic Spirituality*, edited by Michael Downey, 565–77. Collegeville, MN: Liturgical Press, 1993.

Campbell, Mike. "Mary." Behind the Name: The Etymology and History of First Names. (Copyright 1996–2010). No pages. Online: http://www.behindthename.com /name/mary.

Casaldáliga, Pedro, y José María Vigil. *Espiritualidad de la liberación*. Santander: Sal Terrae, 1992.

Catechism of the Catholic Church. Online: http://www.vatican.va/archive/ccc_css /archive/catechism/ccc_toc.htm.

Cavazos-González, Gilberto, OFM. "Cara y Corazón (Face and Heart): Toward a U.S. Latino Spirituality of Inculturation." *New Theology Review* 17 (2004) 46–55.

———. *Clara de Asís: Alter Christus: El tema de la liberación en su Proceso de Canonización*. Roma: Pontificium Atenaeum Antonianum, 1996.

———. "La Cotidianidad Divina: A Latin@ Method for Spirituality." *Journal of Hispanic/ Latino Theology* (2008). No pages. Online: http://www.latinotheology.org/2008 /latinoa_method_spirituality.

———. "The Five Pillars of Liberation Spirituality" *New Theology Review* 18 (2005) 82–85.

———. "Liberation Spirituality and the Process of Canonization for St. Clare of Assisi." *Cord* 52 (July/August 2002) 142–52.

———. "A Spirituality of Study" *New Theology Review* 20 (2007) 70–77.

CELAM. *Documento Conclusivo Aparecida: V Conferencia General*. 2d ed. Aparecida, 2007. Online: http://www.celam.org/celam.info/download/Documento_ Conclusivo_Aparecida.pdf.

———. *Puebla: La evangelización en el presente y en el futuro de América Latina*. 2d ed. Madrid: BAC Minor, 1979.

Ciobotea, Dan-Ilie. "Salvation: The Orthodox Position." In *The Encyclopedia of Christianity*, edited by Erwin Fahlbusch, Geoffrey William Bromiley, and David B. Barrett, 4:822–23. Grand Rapids: Eerdmans, 1999.

Colombas, Gracia M. *Diálogo com Deus: Introdução à "Lectio Divina."* Paulus: São Paulo, 1996.

Dalton, Frederick John. *The Moral Vision of César Chávez*. Maryknoll, NY: Orbis Books, 2003.

De Anasagasti, Pedro. *Liberación en San Francisco de Asís: Peculiar metodología misionera franciscana en el siglo XIII*. Oñate: Editorial Franciscana Aranzazu, 1976.

Diaz, Miguel H. "Life-Giving Migrations: Re-visioning the Mystery of God through U.S. Hispanic Eyes." *Journal of Hispanic/Latino Theology* (2006). No pages. Online: http://www.latinotheology.org/2006/migrations.

Downey, Michael. *Understanding Christian Spirituality*. Mahwah, NJ: Paulist Press, 1997.

Dube, Musa W. "Who Do You Say that I Am?" *Feminist Theology* 15 (2007) 346–67.

Dunne, John. "Meditation XVII." Devotions on Emergent Occasions. In *The Norton Anthology of English Literature*, 4th ed., 1:1108-9. New York: W. W. Norton, 1962.

Elizondo, Virgilio. *Galilean Journey: The Mexican-American Promise*. 2nd ed. Maryknoll, NY: Orbis Books, 2000.

Espín, Orlando O. *The Faith of the People: Theological Reflections on Popular Catholicism*. Maryknoll, NY: Orbis Books, 1997.

———. "Logos/Word." In *An Introductory Dictionary of Theology and Religious Studies*, edited by Orlando O. Espín and James B. Nickoloff, 786. Collegeville, MN: Liturgical Press, 2007.

———. "Mission of the Church." In *An Introductory Dictionary of Theology and Religious Studies*, edited by Orlando O. Espín and James B. Nickoloff, 884–85. Collegeville, MN: Liturgical Press, 2007.

Fine, Alvin. "Life Is a Journey." As quoted by Irwin Wiener, "The Journey to a Promise," in *Jewish News of Greater Phoenix*. No pages. Online: http://www.jewishaz.com /issues/ story.mv?060526+torah.

Fragomeni, Richard N. "Conversion." In *The New Dictionary of Catholic Spirituality*, edited by Michael Downey. Collegeville, MN: Liturgical Press, 1993.

Frohlich, Mary. "Spiritual Discipline, Discipline of Spirituality: Revisiting Questions of Definition and Method." *Spiritus: A Journal of Christian Spirituality* 1 (Spring 2001) 65–78.

Galilea, Segundo. *El seguimiento de Cristo*. 9th ed. Bogota: Ediciones Paulinas, 2006.

Goizueta, Roberto S. "The Christology of Jon Sobrino." In *Hope and Solidarity: Jon Sobrino's Challenge to Christian Theology*, edited by Stephen J. Pope. Maryknoll, NY: Orbis Books, 2008.

Gutiérrez, Gustavo. *A Theology of Liberation: History, Politics and Salvation*. 15th Anniversary edition. Maryknoll, NY: Orbis Books, 1988.

Haase, Albert, OFM. *Living the Lord's Prayer: The Way of the Disciple*. Chicago: InterVarsity Press, 2009.

Hayes, Diana L. "To Be the Bridge: Voices from the Margin." In *A Dream Unfinished: Theological Reflections on America from the Margins*, edited by Eleazar S. Fernandez and Fernando F. Segovia, 52–71. Maryknoll, NY: Orbis Books, 2001.

Hayes, Zachary, OFM. *Hidden Center: Spirituality and Speculative Christology in St. Bonaventure*. St. Bonaventure, NY: The Franciscan Institute, 1994, reprint 2000.

Hellmann, J. A. Wayne. "Social Justice: Gospel Witness and Mission of the Church." In *Theological Foundations: Concepts and Methods for Understanding Christian Faith*, edited by J. J. Mueller et al. Winona, MN: St. María's Press, 2007.

Holmes, Urban T. *A History of Christian Spirituality*. Harrisburg, PA: Morehouse Publishing, 2002.

Hughes, Alfred. *Spiritual Masters: Living a Life of Prayer in the Catholic Tradition*. Huntington, IN: Our Sunday Visitor, 1998.

Interlinear Scripture Analyzer (ISA). "The Greek Interlinear New Testament." In *Scripture 4 All*. No pages. Online: http://www.scripture4all.org/OnlineInterlinear /NTpdf/luk1.pdf.

Iriarte, Lazaro, OFM Cap. *Vocación Franciscana*. Valencia: Editorial Asís, 1989.

Jelly, Frederick M. "Mary and the Church." In *The Gift of the Church: A Textbook on Ecclesiology in Honor of Patrick Granfield*, edited by Peter C. Phan, 435–58. Collegeville, MN: Liturgical Press, 2000.

John Paul II. *Crossing the Threshold of Hope*. New York: Knopf, 1995.

Johnson, Elizabeth A. *Truly Our Sister: A Theology of Mary in the Communion of Saints*. New York: Continuum, 2006.

Katoppo, Marianne. "Poor Mother Earth, Your Children Treat You Like Dirt." *The Jakarta Post*, April 22, 2005. Online: http://www.thejakartapost.com/news/2005/04/22 /poor-mother-earth-your-children-treat-you-dirt.html.

Kreitzer, Beth. *Reforming Mary: Changing Images of the Virgin Mary in Lutheran Sermons of the Sixteenth Century*. New York: Oxford University Press, 2004.

Lawrence, Richard T. "Conversion, II (Theology of)." In *The New Catholic Encyclopedia* [2d ed.], edited by Berard L. Marthaler et al., 4:234–38. Washington, DC: Gale, 2003.

Leo XIII. *Divinum munus illud.* Vatican Papal Archive. Libreria Editrice Vaticana, 1897. No pages. Online: http://www.vatican.va/holy_father/leo_xiii/encyclicals /documents/hf_l-xiii_enc_ 09051897_divinum-illud-munus _en.html.

Marcel, Gabriel. *Homo Viator: Introduction to the Metaphysics of Hope.* Southbend, IN: St. Augustine's Press, 2008.

Matthey, Jacques. "Luke 4:16–30 The Spirit's Mission Manifesto: Jesus' Hermeneutics— and Luke's Editorial." *International Review for Mission* 89, no. 352 (2000). No pages. Online: http://www.sedos.org/english/matthey.html.

Moioli, Giovanni. "Teologia spirituale." In *Nuovo dizionario di spiritualità.* A cura di Stefano De Fiores e Tullio Goffi, 1602, 1608. Cinisello Balsamo (Mi): Edizioni San Paolo, 1999.

Moloney, Francis J. "Conversion, I (The Bible)." In *The New Catholic Encyclopedia* [2d ed.], edited by Berard L. Marthaler et al., 4:232–34. Washington, DC: Gale, 2003.

Nanko-Fernández, Carmen. "From Pajaro to Paraclete: Retrieving the Spirit of God in the Company of Mary." *Journal of Hispanic/Latino Theology* (2007). No pages. Online: http://latinotheology.com/2007/company_of_mary.

———. "Lo Cotidiano." In *Hispanic American Religious Cultures,* edited by Miguel A. De La Torre, 1:158–60. Santa Barbara, CA: ABC-CLIO, 2009.

———. "Theologizing en Espanglish: The Imago Dei in the Vernacular." *Journal of Hispanic/Latino Theology* (2009). No pages. Online: http://www.latinotheology. org/2009/ image_dei_vernacular#_ednref5.

Nolan, Robert B. "Introductory Remarks on the Occasion of Martin Luther King, Jr. Day 2008." *Embassy of the United States: Maseru-Lesotho.* No pages. Online: http: //maseru.usembassy.gov /january_22.html.

Payton, James R. *Light from the Christian East: An Introduction to the Orthodox Tradition.* Downers Grove, IL: InterVarsity Press, 2007.

Pennington, M. Basil, OCSO. "Wisdom." In *The New Dictionary of Catholic Spirituality,* edited by Michael Downey, 1042–43. Collegeville, MN: Liturgical Press, 1993.

Peters, Bosco. "Magnificat (As used by the Cistercians of Tarawara [Australia] and Kopua [New Zealand])." *Liturgy: Worship that Works—Spirituality that Connects.* (2007). No pages. Online: http://www.liturgy.co.nz/resources/magnificat.html.

Pinn, Anthony B. "Jesus and Justice: An Outline of Liberation Theology within Black Churches." *CrossCurrents* (2007). No pages. Online: http://www.questia.com /PM.qst?a=o&d= 5023469491.

Pius XI. "Rerum omnium perturbationem: Encyclical on St. Francis de Sales." Vatican Papal Archive. Libreria Editrice Vaticana, 1923. No pages. Online: http://www. vatican.va/holy_father/pius_xi/encyclicals/ documents/hf_p-xi_enc_26011923_ rerum -omnium-perturbationem_en.html.

Ratzinger, Joseph. *The God of Jesus Christ: Meditations on the Triune God.* San Francisco: Ignatius Press, 2008.

Reid, Barbara E., OP. *Taking Up the Cross: New Testament Interpretations through Latina and Feminist Eyes.* Minneapolis: Fortress, 2007.

Rieman, T. Wayne. "Spirituality: God's Order of Being (Toward Defining Spirituality)." *Brethren Life and Thought* 34, no. 2 (March 1, 1989) 73–81. *ATLA Religion Database with ATLASerials,* EBSCOhost.

Romero, Oscar. "La esperanza cristiana, clave y fuerza de nuestra verdadera liberación." *Servicios Koinonia* (Julio 1977). No pages. Online: http://www.servicioskoinonia .org/romero/ homilias/B/791118.htm.

―――. "Pentecostés: Cumpleaños de la Iglesia." *Servicios Koinonia* (Pentecostés 1978). No pages. Online: http://www.servicioskoinonia.org/romero/homilías/A/780514.htm.

―――. "Por su alianza, Dios nos adopta en su misma familia." *Servicios Koinonia* (Junio 1979). No pages. Online: http://www.servicioskoinonia.org/romero/homilias/B/790610.htm.

Ruiz, Raúl Gómez. *Mozarabs, Hispanics and the Cross.* Maryknoll, NY: Orbis Books, 2007.

Secondin, Bruno. *Spiritualitá in dialogo: Nuovi scenari dell'esperienza spirituale.* Milan: Paoline Editoriale Libri, 1997.

Schmiedel, Paul W. "Mary." In *Encyclopedia Biblica,* edited by T. K. Cheyne and J. Sutherland Black, 3:2952–71. London: Adam and Charles Black, 1902.

Schneiders, Sandra M. "Spirituality in the Academy." *Theological Studies* 50, no. 4 (December 1, 1989) 676–97. *ATLA Religion Database with ATLASerials,* EBSCO*host.*

Schwartz, Arthur. "Growing Spiritually during the College Years." *Liberal Education* 87, no. 4. (2001) 30+. Online: http://www.questia.com/PM.qst?a=o&d=5002438457.

Sobrino, Jon. *Liberación con Espíritu: Apuntes para una nueva espiritualidad.* Santander: Sal Terrae, 1985.

―――. *Spirituality of Liberation: Toward Political Holiness.* Maryknoll, NY: Orbis Books, 1988.

Spiteris, Yannis. *La vita cristiana: Experienza de liberta.* Bologna: EDB, 1993.

Sullivan, Maureen. *101 Questions and Answers on Vatican II.* Mahwah, NJ: Paulist Press, 2003.

Tanquerey, Adolphe. *The Spiritual Life: A Treatise on Ascetical and Mystical Theology.* 2d ed. Rockford, IL: Tan Books and Publishers, 2000.

USCCB. "Popular Devotional Practices: Basic Questions and Answers." Washington, DC: United States Conference of Catholic Bishops, 2003. No pages. Online: http://www.usccb.org/bishops/devprac.shtml.

―――. *Sharing Catholic Social Teaching: Challenges and Directions: Reflections of the U.S. Catholic Bishops.* Washington, DC: USCCB Publishing, 1998. No pages. Online: http://www.usccb.org/sdwp/projects/socialteaching/socialteaching.shtml.

Walck, Leslie W. "The Son of Man in the Parables of Enoch and the Gospels." In *Enoch and the Messiah Son of Man: Revisiting the Book of Parables,* edited by Gabriele Boccaccini and Jason von Ehrenkrook, 299–337. Grand Rapids: Eerdmans, 2007.

Ward, Thomas. "From the 'People' to the 'Nation': An Emerging Notion in Sahagún, Ixtlilxóchitl." *E-Journal: Estudios de Cultura Nahuatl* (2001) 223–34. Online: http://www. ejournal.unam.mx/ecn/ecnahuatl32/ECN03212.pdf.

Warner, Keith Douglass, OFM. "The Farm Workers and the Franciscans: Reverse Evangelization as Social Prompt for Conversion." *Spiritus: A Journal of Christian Spirituality* 9, no. 1 (2009) 69–88.

White, C. Vanessa. "Liturgy as a Liberating Force." In *Liturgy and Justice: To Worship God in Spirit and Truth,* edited by Anne Y. Koester, 109–116. Collegeville, MN: Liturgical Press, 2002.

Whitehead, Evelyn Eaton, and James D. Whitehead. *Seasons of Strength: New Visions of Adult Christian Maturing.* 2d ed. Winona, MN: Saint Mary's Press, 1995.

Subject/Name Index